Exploring
the
Jewish Holidays
and
Customs

Exploring the Jewish Holidays and Customs

by
Shirley Stern

Ktav Publishing House Inc.

To my father, Bernard Gartenstein,
and to Gertie with love and gratitude

ISBN 0-87068-869-3

© COPYRIGHT 1981
KTAV PUBLISHING HOUSE, INC.

MANUFACTURED IN THE UNITED STATES OF AMERICA

TABLE OF CONTENTS

UNIT I

THE JEWISH DAY

Think of a day in your life. You wake up in the morning, go to school, eat breakfast, lunch, and dinner, play with your friends, watch television, read, help with chores, and do many other things. You are busy until it is night and time to go to bed. The next day you wake again to a busy day.

One day follows another. From waking up to going to bed you do many things. You spend time with many people. You experience many things.

What you do each day will depend on who you are, where you live, and what those around you do. You do certain things because you live in a particular neighborhood and a particular coun-try, because you are a particular age, because you are a boy or a girl, because you belong to a family group.

This book is about those special things you do because you are Jewish. Being Jewish is an important part of every day of your life. In this unit, you will learn about some of the everyday things you do or experience because you are a Jewish boy or girl. You will also go back in time, to read about how Jewish holidays and ceremonies were ob-served in the lives of your grandparents and great-grandparents when they were children. And you will be carried thousands of miles to Israel, to see how our Jewish holidays are celebrated in the Jewish homeland.

JEWISH LIFE EVERY DAY

*God said, "Let there be light." And there was light.
And God saw that the light was good; and God divided
the light from the darkness. And God called the light
Day. And the darkness God called Night. And there
was evening and there was morning, one day.*

—Genesis 1:3–5

The alarm clock buzzes. You open one eye and peek out. It is a bright, sunny day. A good day to enjoy. A day on which you can do many things. A day on which you will have many new experiences. You get out of bed eager to start the day. "What kind of day will it be?" you wonder.

Many things happen to each of us in the course of a day. Some things we do and experience because we are uniquely ourselves. We are individuals with our own needs, preferences, and routines. Other things we do and experience because of who we are in relation to others. We are members of a family, and some parts of our daily life are a result of this. We go to school, and do and experience many things there. We have friends, and have special experiences as a result. We are citizens of our country, living in a particular city, town, or region. All of these help to determine what we will do or experience in the course of a day.

In this chapter you will learn about the things you do, and the experiences you have, because you are Jewish.

Many things happened to us in the course of a day. We go to school, we have friends, we go on vacation and have lots of experiences.

9

The pursuit of shalom is an important mitzvah. An art contest was held in Israel in which the children drew pictures of "shalom." The winning drawings were made into Israeli stamps. Here is one of them.

MITZVAH

One of the things that make the Jewish way of life special is the idea of doing mitzvot. The word *mitzvah* means "commandment." Originally it referred only to the commandments in the Bible that tell us how a Jew should live. Sometimes the word is also used in referring to customs and practices that are part of the special Jewish way of life even if not commanded in the Bible.

Basically there are two kinds of mitzvot. Some of them tell us what we *should* do. These are known as "positive commandments," and in Hebrew they are called Mitzvot Aseh ("Mitzvot to do"). Others tell us what we should *not* do. These are known as "negative commandments," and in Hebrew they are called Mitzvot Lo Ta'aseh ("Mitzvot not to do").

The rabbis of the past calculated that there were a total of 613 commandments in the Bible. They called these the Taryag Mitzvot because the Hebrew letters that stand for 613 spell out the word Taryag.

Many of the 613 commandments applied only in ancient times. Others were relevant only in the Land of Israel. Many of them have meaning in all times and places. These are the important mitzvot that deal with our day-to-day lives, our relations with others, and our observance of the practices of the Jewish religion.

Among these important mitzvot are respecting our parents, not killing or stealing, observing Shabbat, and performing such rituals as circumcision. Studying Torah is also a mitzvah. So is celebrating the Jewish holidays and giving *zedakah*. Having a Jewish home is a mitzvah. Going to services in the temple is a mitzvah. There are many other mitzvot that you or your parents perform regularly. How many can you think of?

PRAYERS

Praying is also a very important part of the special Jewish way of life. Prayer services take place in the temple on every Shabbat and holy day. Orthodox synagogues, and Conservative synagogues as well, maintain the old tradition of holding daily prayer services every weekday. Each part of the day has its own prayer service. The morning service is called *shacharit*, the afternoon service is called *mincha*, and the evening service is called *maariv*.

The prayer called *Kaddish* is an important part of every Jewish service. It is said in memory of those who have died. Many Jews go to the temple to recite this special prayer on the anniversary of the death of close relatives. This occasion is called the *Yahrzeit*.

Many Jews wear a prayer shawl called a *tallit* when reciting their prayers *(tefilot)*. The tallit is a reminder of the fringed robe that Jews wore in ancient times. Its fringes are made in accordance with special instructions given in the Bible.

Some Jews also wear *tefilin* during the morning service on weekdays. The tefilin are two small leather boxes with long thongs attached. The thongs are

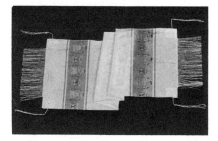

The tallit, or prayer shawl, is donned during the morning (and additional) prayers (on Tisha B'Av in the afternoon, and on Yom Kippur at all services). It is a four-cornered garment, usually made of wool, upon the corners of which tzitzit have been knotted in accordance with the Biblical rules (Numbers 15:37–41).

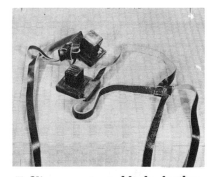

Tefilin are two black leather boxes, fastened to leather straps, containing four portions of the Bible written on parchment (Exodus 13:1–10, 11–16; Deuteronomy 6:4–9; 11:13–21).

We praise God for helping us to bring forth bread from the earth. We thank God for sending the sun and the rain to help growing things spring forth from the earth.

wrapped around the head and arm to hold the box in place. Inside each box is a piece of parchment with a verse from the Torah. The ceremony of putting on tefilin is a reminder of the verse from the Bible that says, "You shall bind them (reminders of God's law) for a sign upon your hand, and they shall be for frontlets between your eyes."

Another old custom is to wear something on one's head when praying. In ancient times covering the head was a way of showing respect.

BLESSINGS

In addition to the temple services on Shabbat and holy days, there are prayers of a different kind that can be recited from time to time throughout the day, wherever you are. These are *blessings (b'rachot)* and prayers of thanksgiving. Jewish tradition includes blessings for all sorts of occasions. See how many you already know. Then see how many new ones you can learn.

Many families begin their meals by saying:

I praise God, who is Lord and Ruler over all,
for bringing forth bread from the earth.

בָּרוּךְ אַתָּה יְיָ, אֱלֹהֵינוּ מֶלֶךְ הָעוֹלָם, הַמּוֹצִיא לֶחֶם מִן הָאָרֶץ.

They conclude the meal by saying Grace, which ends with the blessing:

I praise God for the food which has been given to all.

בָּרוּךְ אַתָּה יְיָ הַזָּן אֶת הַכֹּל.

12

The blessing for wine is:

I praise God, who is Lord and Ruler over all,
for creating the grapes of the vine.

בָּרוּךְ אַתָּה יְיָ, אֱלֹהֵינוּ מֶלֶךְ הָעוֹלָם, בּוֹרֵא
פְּרִי הַגָּפֶן.

When we eat fruit we say:

I praise God, who is Lord and Ruler over all,
for making the fruit of the tree.

בָּרוּךְ אַתָּה יְיָ, אֱלֹהֵינוּ מֶלֶךְ הָעוֹלָם, בּוֹרֵא
פְּרִי הָעֵץ.

The blessing when something special happens is:

I praise God, who is Lord and Ruler over all,
for keeping us well to reach this season.

בָּרוּךְ אַתָּה יְיָ, אֱלֹהֵינוּ מֶלֶךְ הָעוֹלָם, שֶׁהֶחֱיָנוּ
וְקִיְּמָנוּ וְהִגִּיעָנוּ לַזְּמַן הַזֶּה.

Thanking God by saying these blessings helps us to appreciate all the good things that are part of our lives and that we would otherwise take for granted.

DIETARY LAWS

Another way in which many Jews make being Jewish a part of their daily lives is by observing some or all of the many food practices and customs known as the Dietary Laws, or laws of *kashrut*.

Jews have had special food practices since ancient times. The Bible prohibits the eating of pork products and shellfish. Blood is also forbidden. The rabbis and

Shehitah ("slaughtering") of animals is carried out in accordance with humane Jewish laws. Only a properly qualified person, called a shohet, may perform shehitah. The meat is then inspected and certified as kosher. The kosher stamp shown here was used in a European Jewish community in the nineteenth century.

13

In 1565, Joseph Karo compiled the Shulchan Aruch. Joseph Karo studied all the discussions of Jewish law and printed the decisions in his book. The Shulchan Aruch is a guide for the observance of traditional Judaism. Reform and Conservative Judaism observe many of these laws. This Israeli stamp was issued in honor of the Shulchan Aruch.

sages, building upon the Biblical commandments, added other details. Meat products may not be mixed with dairy products. Meat is only kosher if it comes from animals that are slaughtered in a special way. Eggs with specks of blood in them may not be eaten, and fruits and vegetables in which a worm is found must be discarded.

Some Jews still observe these laws very strictly, but most Reform Jews believe that the dietary laws are no longer an important part of being Jewish. Other Reform Jews observe some of them but not all. Still others say that vegetarianism is an important part of being Jewish. What does your family do?

The traditions and practices described in this chapter are only some of the ways in which you can make your life uniquely Jewish. Some Jews find these practices helpful and consider them very important. Others do not. But even so there are many things that make their lives Jewish. They go to Jewish schools. They read books of Jewish interest. They give zedakah. They have Jewish friends. They belong to a temple. They are concerned about the Jews in Israel and all over the world. They have a special feeling about being Jewish. All of these things make being Jewish an important part of your daily life. All of these things help to make your life different from the lives of those who are not Jewish.

FOCUS ON THE CONCEPT: ZEDAKAH

The Hebrew word *zedakah* is sometimes translated as "charity," but it really means "righteousness," or doing the right thing. The Jewish idea of zedakah goes much further than the idea of charity. In the Jewish view, it is not merely enough to help someone in need. It is also important to help in the kindest way possible, so as to protect the feelings of the person being helped. Best of all, you should help in such a way that the person can become self-supporting and no longer need charity. By making the recipient of charity independent, you perform the mitzvah of restoring his or her human dignity.

Moses Maimonides was one of the greatest Jewish thinkers. He illustrated this point by listing a series of levels of zedakah. All of the levels are good, because all represent ways of helping people in need, but some levels are better than others. Read Maimonides' levels of zedakah and see whether they help you to understand the difference between zedakah and charity.

By contributing to our local Federation, we nourish all the agencies on the Federation roster. Thus we aid Jewish education, hospitals, the poor and the aged, summer camps, and many other causes. This photo was taken at the 92nd Street Y in New York, the largest and most famous community center in the world and a member agency of New York's Federation of Jewish Philanthropies.

A drawing of Rabbi Moses Maimonides. His Hebrew name was Rabbi Moshe ben Maimon. We lovingly call him Rambam. The name Rambam comes from the Hebrew letters R-Rabbi, M-Moshe, B-Ben, M-Maimon.

משֶׁה בּרבּי מיימון זצ״ל

The autograph of Maimonides.

LEVELS OF ZEDAKAH

1. You give charity to someone, but only because it is your duty, not because you really want to.

2. You really want to help, because you know it is the right thing to do, but you don't give as much as the person needs.

3. You give cheerfully, because you know it is the right thing to do, and you give enough, but you don't give until the person has to undergo the embarrassment of asking you for help.

4. You give cheerfully, and enough, and before you are asked, but you give it directly to the person, thus causing him or her to be embarrassed.

5. You give cheerfully, and enough, and before you are asked, and you do it in such a way that you do not know who receives the zedakah, so that there is no way for you to embarrass or take advantage of the recipient.

6. You give cheerfully, and enough, and before you are asked, and you do it in such a way that the person who receives the zedakah does not know who gave it, and thus does not have to feel embarrassed in your presence.

7. You do not know the identity of the person helped, and he or she does not know that you provided the zedakah; thus the recipient is not embarrassed and there is no way for you to take advantage of your generosity.

8. This is the highest level: you don't simply give money or other aid, but do something to enable the recipient to become self-supporting—for example, by providing a job or training—so that he or she will become independent and never again have to depend upon others for help.

SOMETHING TO THINK ABOUT

There are many things that you and your family do in your daily lives that are especially Jewish. What are some of the things that you yourself do? How do you feel about doing them?

SHARING VALUES

Make a list of all the especially Jewish things you and your family do. Check the three you value the most. Share how you feel about these things with a friend in class.

HEBREW WORDS AND PHRASES

Below is a list of Hebrew words and phrases relating to Jewish life every day. See how many you can learn.

מִצְוָה	Mitzvah	A good deed, commandment
שַׁחֲרִית	Shacharit	The morning service
מִנְחָה	Mincha	The afternoon service
מַעֲרִיב	Maariv	The evening service
תְּפִילָה	Tefilah	Prayer
תְּפִילִין	Tefilin	Leather boxes containing parchments, worn on head and arms during morning prayers
טַלִּית	Tallit	Prayer shawl
כַּשְׁרוּת	Kashrut	Dietary laws
בְּרָכוֹת	B'rachot	Blessings
צְדָקָה	Zedakah	Charity, righteousness
קַדִּישׁ	Kaddish	Prayer in memory of those who have died

THE JEWISH HOME

From of old our homes have been the dwelling place of the Jewish spirit. Within their walls our ancestors built altars of faith and love. There they maintained the habit of daily devotion; there they prepared a table for the stranger and the needy.

—Rabbi's Manual

Most Jews attend services at their temple. Some attend often and others just once in a while. While the temple is very important, it is not the real center of Jewish life. Jewish life really centers around the home. Close family life is an important Jewish value, and most Jews enjoy their homes, and the peace and contentment they find there.

A SMALL SANCTUARY

The Jewish home has been called a small sanctuary because many religious rituals are observed there. In most religions, religious events happen only in a special place, such as a church, a mosque, or a temple. But Jews observe many of their religious traditions at home. There are special home rituals for celebrating Shabbat and each holiday. Many holidays start the evening before with a festive meal. Candles are lit and blessed. Kiddush is recited and a blessing said over the challah.

Each holiday has its special foods and customs. There are dairy foods for Shavuot, and latkes, or potato pancakes, for Chanukah. There are apples and honey for Rosh Hashana, and hamantaschen for Purim. On Sukkot, meals are eaten in the sukkah. On Shavuot, the home is decorated with flowers and greens. On Passover, there is a Seder. On Chanukah, candles are lit and placed in the window. These and other customs are observed in the home. Celebrating the holidays together and sharing religious experiences helps to bring family members closer together.

In many Jewish homes it is traditional for the parent to bless the children on Friday night. For boys the blessing is, "May God make you like Ephraim and Manasseh." For girls it is, "May God make you like Sarah, Rebecca, Rachel, and Leah."
This painting by the artist Moritz Oppenheim illustrates a blessing scene in a German Jewish home. This picture was painted in about 1850.

The Jewish home has been called a small sanctuary because many religious rituals are observed there.

19

A painting by the artist Marc Chagall.

When Jews pray, they face towards Jerusalem. The Mizrach reminds us in which direction to pray.

JEWISH ART

During some periods of Jewish history, Jews did not believe in having works of art in their homes, especially works of art that showed people or animals. They believed that these were like the graven images forbidden by the Second Commandment. But most Jews do not believe this any more. There are many Jewish artists who portray Jewish subjects, and many Jews have Jewish paintings and sculptures in their homes. Some of the well-known Jewish artists who have used Jewish themes are Marc Chagall, Raymond Katz, Alfred Van Loen, Irving Amen, Ezekiel Schloss, and Morton Garchik.

THE MIZRACH

A special kind of Jewish painting is called a *mizrach*. The mizrach (which means "east" in Hebrew) is a painting or plaque with a Jewish theme that is used to mark the eastern wall of the home. Whenever Jews pray, either at the temple or at home, they face east. This is the direction of Jerusalem. The mizrach is a symbol of the importance of Jerusalem and Israel to all Jews. It is also a reminder that daily prayers may be recited at home as well as in the temple.

THE JEWISH HOME BEAUTIFUL

Many Jewish homes can be recognized by the special Jewish objects contained in them. These include ritual objects, such as Sabbath candlesticks, a Kiddush cup, a chanukia, a Seder plate, and others. They also include paintings and sculptures with Jewish themes and books on Jewish subjects.

JEWISH BOOKS

The Jews have been called the "People of the Book." Reading and studying have always been important Jewish values. Many books are written each year on Jewish subjects, and most Jewish homes have at least some books of Jewish interest.

Almost every Jewish home has copies of the Bible and the Sabbath and holiday prayerbooks. Many also have Jewish history books, biographies of famous Jews, books about Jewish customs, and novels on Jewish themes.

There are many present-day authors who write on Jewish subjects. Some of them are Elie Wiesel, who writes moving novels about the Holocaust; Harry Kemelman, a detective-story writer, whose detective hero is a New England rabbi; and Isaac Bashevis Singer, winner of a Nobel Prize for Literature.

THE MEZUZAH

One way to identify almost any Jewish home, anywhere in the world, is by the mezuzah on the door. The

Jewish books and religious objects grace a Jewish home.

The mezuzah ("doorpost") is a parchment scroll placed in a container and nailed to the doorpost. On the scroll is written Deuteronomy 6:4–9 and 11:13–21. The silver mezuzah shown here was made in Germany, about 1805.

שְׁמַע יִשְׂרָאֵל יְהֹוָה אֱלֹהֵינוּ יְהֹוָה אֶחָד וְאָהַבְתָּ אֵת
יְהֹוָה אֱלֹהֶיךָ בְּכָל לְבָבְךָ וּבְכָל נַפְשְׁךָ וּבְכָל מְאֹדֶךָ וְהָיוּ
הַדְּבָרִים הָאֵלֶּה אֲשֶׁר אָנֹכִי מְצַוְּךָ הַיּוֹם עַל לְבָבֶךָ וְשִׁנַּנְתָּם
לְבָנֶיךָ וְדִבַּרְתָּ בָּם בְּשִׁבְתְּךָ בְּבֵיתֶךָ וּבְלֶכְתְּךָ בַדֶּרֶךְ
וּבְשָׁכְבְּךָ וּבְקוּמֶךָ וּקְשַׁרְתָּם לְאוֹת עַל יָדֶךָ וְהָיוּ לְטֹטָפֹת
בֵּין עֵינֶיךָ וּכְתַבְתָּם עַל מְזוּזֹת בֵּיתֶךָ וּבִשְׁעָרֶיךָ
וְהָיָה אִם שָׁמֹעַ תִּשְׁמְעוּ אֶל מִצְוֺתַי אֲשֶׁר אָנֹכִי
מְצַוֶּה אֶתְכֶם הַיּוֹם לְאַהֲבָה אֶת יְהֹוָה אֱלֹהֵיכֶם וּלְעָבְדוֹ
בְּכָל לְבַבְכֶם וּבְכָל נַפְשְׁכֶם וְנָתַתִּי מְטַר אַרְצְכֶם בְּעִתּוֹ
יוֹרֶה וּמַלְקוֹשׁ וְאָסַפְתָּ דְגָנֶךָ וְתִירֹשְׁךָ וְיִצְהָרֶךָ וְנָתַתִּי
עֵשֶׂב בְּשָׂדְךָ לִבְהֶמְתֶּךָ וְאָכַלְתָּ וְשָׂבָעְתָּ הִשָּׁמְרוּ לָכֶם
פֶּן יִפְתֶּה לְבַבְכֶם וְסַרְתֶּם וַעֲבַדְתֶּם אֱלֹהִים אֲחֵרִים
וְהִשְׁתַּחֲוִיתֶם לָהֶם וְחָרָה אַף יְהֹוָה בָּכֶם וְעָצַר אֶת
הַשָּׁמַיִם וְלֹא יִהְיֶה מָטָר וְהָאֲדָמָה לֹא תִתֵּן אֶת יְבוּלָהּ
וַאֲבַדְתֶּם מְהֵרָה מֵעַל הָאָרֶץ הַטֹּבָה אֲשֶׁר יְהֹוָה נֹתֵן לָכֶם
וְשַׂמְתֶּם אֶת דְּבָרַי אֵלֶּה עַל לְבַבְכֶם וְעַל נַפְשְׁכֶם וּקְשַׁרְתֶּם
אֹתָם לְאוֹת עַל יֶדְכֶם וְהָיוּ לְטוֹטָפֹת בֵּין עֵינֵיכֶם וְלִמַּדְתֶּם
אֹתָם אֶת בְּנֵיכֶם לְדַבֵּר בָּם בְּשִׁבְתְּךָ בְּבֵיתֶךָ וּבְלֶכְתְּךָ
בַדֶּרֶךְ וּבְשָׁכְבְּךָ וּבְקוּמֶךָ וּכְתַבְתָּם עַל מְזוּזוֹת בֵּיתֶךָ
וּבִשְׁעָרֶיךָ לְמַעַן יִרְבּוּ יְמֵיכֶם וִימֵי בְנֵיכֶם עַל הָאֲדָמָה
אֲשֶׁר נִשְׁבַּע יְהֹוָה לַאֲבֹתֵיכֶם לָתֵת לָהֶם כִּימֵי הַשָּׁמַיִם
עַל הָאָרֶץ

The mezuzah scroll contains the Shema.
The Shema Yisrael ("Hear, O Israel") is Judaism's confession of faith, proclaiming the absolute unity of God. It consists of three quotations from the Bible: Deuteronomy 6:4–9, 11:13–21; Numbers 15:37–41.

mezuzah is a tiny box nailed to the right-hand side of the doorpost. Inside is a small handwritten parchment scroll containing the words in Hebrew: "You shall write them (the words of the Torah) upon the doorposts of your house and upon your gates." The mezuzah on the door represents the desire of the family who lives inside to follow the teachings of Judaism and the Torah.

Mezuzot can be either plain or decorative. Some of them have been designed by artists and are very beautiful. But what is most important are the words inside. Many Jews consider the mezuzah and what it symbolizes so important that they kiss the mezuzah as they leave or enter the home.

When a mezuzah is first placed on the door of a home a special prayer is said:

I praise God, who is Lord and Ruler over all, who made us special by commanding us to put up a mezuzah.

בָּרוּךְ אַתָּה יְיָ אֱלֹהֵינוּ מֶלֶךְ הָעוֹלָם, אֲשֶׁר קִדְּשָׁנוּ בְּמִצְוֹתָיו וְצִוָּנוּ לִקְבֹּעַ מְזוּזָה.

The mezuzah is usually placed on the door when the family first moves into the home. Often this takes place at a special ceremony called Chanukat Habayit (Dedication of the Home). Special prayers are said, and friends are invited to share in the festivities.

In what way is your home different from the homes of your non-Jewish friends? Does your family do special things because it is Jewish? Would a stranger coming into your home recognize that it is a Jewish home? How?

SHARING AN EXPERIENCE

Prepare a traditional Jewish holiday food at home. Bring it to school and share it with your classmates. Be prepared to tell on what holiday your family usually eats this food. Describe to your classmates how the food is prepared.

HEBREW WORDS AND PHRASES

Below is a list of Hebrew words and phrases relating to the Jewish home. See how many you can learn.

מִזְרָח	Mizrach	"East," a plaque marking the eastern wall of a Jewish home
מְזוּזָה	Mezuzah	A parchment scroll attached to the right-hand side of the doorpost
קִדּוּשׁ	Kiddush	Ceremony of blessing wine at the beginning of Shabbat and festivals
הַבְדָּלָה	Havdalah	"Separation," the ceremony at the end of Shabbat
בְּשָׂמִים	Besamim	Spices
חֲנוּכִּיָה	Chanukia	Eight-branched candelabra used only on Chanukah
קְעָרָה	Karah	Compartmented plate used at Passover Seder
שְׁטֶעטְל	Shtetl	European Jewish village

Long ago, in the days of your grandparents and great-grandparents, many Jews lived in small Jewish villages in Eastern Europe. Such a village was called a "shtetl." Although life was very hard for the people there, it is remembered as a special time in Jewish history. Since almost all the people who lived in these villages were Jewish, Jewish life was very strong. The children attended Jewish schools. All the Jewish holidays were celebrated. When speaking to each other, the Jews used their own language, Yiddish. They had very little contact with their non-Jewish neighbors. Sometimes they conducted business with them, but there were few friendships between Jews and non-Jews. The non-Jews did not influence the Jewish life-style.

Life in the shtetl revolved around being Jewish. This is very hard for us to understand. We live in a free country. There are Jews and non-Jews in our towns and cities. Our homes are on

For six days in the week the Jews of the shtetl toiled and sweated for their bread. Shabbat was devoted to prayer, study, and family. In this photograph, we see a proud father and mother reviewing their son's progress in the cheder (Hebrew school).

streets where non-Jews as well as Jews live. We speak English. We go to schools with non-Jews. We have non-Jewish friends. The way we live is not really that much different from the way our non-Jewish friends live. The only difference is that we follow our religion and they follow theirs. But the shtetl was different.

The life of the shtetl no longer exists anywhere. The Holocaust changed that. (You will read more about that when you read about Yom Hashoah on page 156.) But we are still interested in knowing about life in the shtetl. It helps us to understand more about our religion. It also helps us to understand our roots. From time to time there will be sections in this book telling about the shtetl and how Jewish customs were followed there. From them you will learn to understand something about Jewish life in the days of your grandparents and great-grandparents.

Three generations of a European Jewish family: grandparents, parents, and grandchildren. Notice the clothing changes in the different generations.

UNIT II
THE JEWISH WEEK

Our days are organized into weeks, units of time each having seven days. A week has five or six working days and a weekend of one or two days when we do not work. We take this for granted. But it was not always so. There is nothing natural about a seven-day week. A day is a natural unit of time. It is the time from sunrise to sunrise—the time it takes for the earth to rotate once on its axis. A month is a natural unit of time. It is the time from new moon to new moon. (You will read more about this on page 48.) A year is a natural unit of time. It is the time it takes the earth to revolve around the sun.

But the week is not a natural unit of time. It had to be invented. Many scholars believe that the Jews invented the seven-day week ending with Shabbat, a day of rest. We read in the Bible that God created the world in six days. On the seventh day, Shabbat, God rested. That was the first week. Next time that you are enjoying a weekend, remember that it would not exist if the Jews had not invented the week.

In this unit you will learn about the Jewish week. You will learn about some of the special things that Jews do each week.

SHABBAT

Once, long ago, a rich and powerful king and a wise but poor rabbi were friends. One Friday evening, the rabbi invited the king to his humble home for Shabbat dinner. The king shared the simple meal with the rabbi and his family. Never had he enjoyed such a delightful dinner. "I want my cook to learn to prepare a meal just like this," he said to the rabbi.

The rabbi taught the king's cook how to make all the delicious foods they had both enjoyed in the rabbi's home. But when the dinner was prepared, it was not the same. Something was missing.

"I think I know what is wrong," said the rabbi to the king. "The meal you ate at my home was a Shabbat meal. The missing secret ingredient in the meal you served me was the spirit of Shabbat."

—Midrash

It is Friday afternoon—the end of a hard week at school. The dismissal bell rings. You pick up your books and walk to the door. "Thank goodness, it's Friday," you say to yourself as you head for home. "I really need some time off to rest and refresh myself."

We all look forward to a day of rest at the end of a week of work. We take it for granted that that is how it should be. But long, long ago, before you or your parents or grandparents or even great-grandparents were born—thousands of years ago—there was no such thing as a day of rest. Then came *Shabbat*. The idea of a day set aside for rest was one of the greatest gifts the Jews gave the world.

SHABBAT IN THE BIBLE

We first learn about Shabbat at the very beginning of the Bible, in the Book of Genesis. There, the story of the creation of the world is told. God created the world in six days. First God created the heaven and the earth. Next God created water and dry land. Then God made the sun, the moon, and the stars, fish and birds and animals. Finally God created people. When all the work was finished, on the seventh day, God rested. God blessed the seventh day, making it special because that was the day of resting from all the work of creation.

Further on in the Bible, in the Book of Exodus, are the Ten Commandments. They tell us what we must do and what is right. The Fourth Commandment tells us that just as God rested on the seventh day, which is Shabbat, we too must rest from all our work. Other

A ninth-century Persian Shabbat lamp.

28

Jewish holy days are mentioned in the Bible. But Shabbat is the only one that is in the Ten Commandments.

In other places in the Bible we are told exactly how we can make Shabbat special. We are told that not only may we not work, but the people who work for us may not work. Even animals may not do any work on Shabbat. We are told that we may not light fires on Shabbat and that our food is to be prepared beforehand. We are also told that observing Shabbat creates a special sign or bond between God and the Jews forever.

SHABBAT IN ANCIENT TIMES

As the centuries passed, different Shabbat customs developed. In ancient times, in Israel, Shabbat was announced by blowing six blasts on the shofar. When the first blast was blown, all the farmers who were working in the fields stopped work and started for home. When the second blast was heard, all the shops were closed. At the third blast, Shabbat candles were lit and blessed in homes all across the country. The last three blasts announced that Shabbat had actually started.

SHABBAT IN THE MIDDLE AGES

In the Middle Ages a very beautiful custom was added to the celebration of Shabbat. The singing of *Zmirot*, or Shabbat songs, was introduced. These lovely songs, which were sung at mealtime, are still sung in many homes. Perhaps your own family enjoys singing Zmirot. Many of the songs that are sung today are the same

Blessings for candle-lighting for Shabbat and holidays, from an eighteenth-century Italian prayer book. Note the interesting Shabbat lamp and the Italian translation.

Shabbat, the day of rest, is ushered in with the lighting of the candles.

songs that were sung many hundreds of years ago.

Other customs were also added at this time. One especially beautiful ceremony was that of welcoming Shabbat. The members of the community would march to the outskirts of the city. There they would wait for Shabbat to arrive. As they waited for darkness to fall and Shabbat to arrive, they would recite prayers and sing hymns.

Still another custom added during the Middle Ages was the blessing of the children of the family on Friday evening. This ceremony is still observed in many homes as part of the Shabbat celebration. You will read more about it later in this chapter.

SHABBAT IN MODERN TIMES

In our own time Shabbat is celebrated in many Jewish homes with festivity and joy. Many special rituals are observed that help make Shabbat a very special day for the entire family.

The celebration of Shabbat begins early on Friday with many special preparations. Although delicious *challah* can be bought in the bakery, many families still enjoy baking their own. Often the entire family participates in mixing the ingredients, kneading the dough, and braiding and shaping the challah. The entire house is especially cleaned for Shabbat, and the table is beautifully set with the prettiest tablecloth and the best dishes. On the table are placed candlesticks and candles, two loaves of challah covered with a special cloth, and a Kiddush cup filled with wine.

On Friday evening Mother lights the Shabbat candles. In some families each daughter lights a candle as well. Then mother covers her eyes and recites the blessing:

I praise God, who is Lord and Ruler over all,
for teaching us the commandment of greeting the
Sabbath by the lighting of candles.

בָּרוּךְ אַתָּה יְיָ, אֱלֹהֵינוּ מֶלֶךְ הָעוֹלָם, אֲשֶׁר
קִדְּשָׁנוּ בְּמִצְוֹתָיו וְצִוָּנוּ לְהַדְלִיק נֵר שֶׁל שַׁבָּת.

These eighteenth-century candle-sticks, made in Germany, have scenes from the Bible on their bases. On the right-hand one Moses is tending sheep.

Mother uncovers her eyes and says "Shabbat Shalom" to everyone.

In many families one or both parents then bless each child. Sometimes a husband will recite a portion from the Book of Proverbs in honor of his wife. The members of the family then sit down to enjoy the Shabbat meal together. The *Kiddush* is recited and everyone joins in the *b'racha* for the wine:

I praise God, who is Lord and Ruler over all, for
creating the grapes of the vine.

בָּרוּךְ אַתָּה יְיָ, אֱלֹהֵינוּ מֶלֶךְ הָעוֹלָם, בּוֹרֵא
פְּרִי הַגָּפֶן.

After everyone takes a sip of wine, they recite the b'racha over the challah together.

I praise God, who is Lord and Ruler over all, for
bringing forth bread from the earth.

בָּרוּךְ אַתָּה יְיָ, אֱלֹהֵינוּ מֶלֶךְ הָעוֹלָם, הַמּוֹצִיא
לֶחֶם מִן־הָאָרֶץ.

Israeli stamp with Shabbat challah cover.

The Shabbat meal is eaten accompanied by lively conversation and the singing of Zmirot.

After dinner, many families attend late Friday evening services at the temple (Bet Knesset). This service is in Hebrew and English, and usually includes a sermon by the rabbi or a lecture by a guest speaker. It is followed by an Oneg Shabbat, a social hour, at which refreshments are served and friends who have not seen each other since the week before get a chance to socialize. The late Friday night service with an Oneg Shabbat afterwards is a modern-day addition to the joyful celebration of Shabbat.

Saturday morning, services are again held at the temple. The Shabbat service is led by a rabbi and a chazan (cantor). The *Torah* is taken from the ark and the Sidrah (portion of the week) is read along with the *Haftarah*. Often there is a *Bar* or *Bat Mitzvah*, and festivities follow the service.

After lunch the day is spent in restful, quiet enjoyment. It is a time for conversation, thinking, and reading. Some families enjoy taking a Shabbat walk.

Finally the sun sets and it is time for Shabbat to end. But it does not end abruptly. Just as Shabbat begins with special ceremonies, so too does it end with a special ritual, a service called Havdalah, or "separation." A Kiddush cup is filled with wine. A spice box is filled with besamim, or sweet-smelling spices, and the braided Havdalah candle is lit. Special blessings are recited. The entire family sings *Eliyahu Hanavi* ("Elijah the Prophet"), and all wish each other Shavua Tov, a good week.

Shabbat is over for another week. Everyone is rested and refreshed and ready to get back to the hustle and bustle of everyday life.

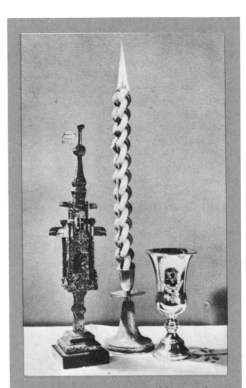

We bid farewell to Shabbat at the Havdalah ceremony, using the spicebox, the braided candle, and the cup of wine.

33

SOMETHING TO THINK ABOUT

A Jewish author wrote: "More than the Jews have preserved Shabbat, Shabbat has preserved the Jews."
  What do you think he meant? Do you agree?

SHARING AN EXPERIENCE

Attend Shabbat services with your family. Tell your classmates about it.

A SPECIAL PROJECT

Make Shabbat candlesticks: Form two balls of self-hardening clay. Shape each into a candlestick. Make a depression in each for a candle. Allow to harden. Paint or spray.

ON YOUR OWN

Read *The Shabbat Catalogue* by Ruth Brin.

LEARNING MORE ABOUT:
SHABBAT IN THE SHTETL

Shabbat in the shtetl had a special flavor. Preparations began on Thursday when people went to market to shop for food. Although most of the people who lived in the shtetl were very poor, and many ate sparingly all week, the very best they could afford was bought for Shabbat. Thursday evening the dough was prepared for challah and left to rise overnight so it could be baked early Friday morning.

On Friday morning, the loaves of dough were placed in large ovens. The Shabbat meal was also prepared at that time. Since no cooking was permitted on Shabbat, all the food had to be prepared in advance. Usually a large pot of stew called chollent was prepared. It was made of meat, potatoes, beans, or other vegetables and allowed to cook in a slow oven overnight. It smelled and tasted delicious.

The children of the shtetl were especially happy when the end of the week came. The schools closed at noon on Friday and did not open again until Sunday morning. The students looked forward to this free time. Life was very hard for children in the shtetl. They were poor. The non-Jews were unfriendly. School hours were very long. The children went to school from early morning to evening and had very little time to play. Is it any wonder that they were so happy when Shabbat came and they could forget their hard life for a while?

In the shtetl, boys and girls were taught separately. A female teacher instructs her pupils.

LEARNING MORE ABOUT:
SHABBAT IN ISRAEL

Shabbat is welcomed in Israel with great ceremony and joy. School ends early so that the children can be at home to help with the preparations. Banks and public offices also close early in honor of Shabbat, and by noon on Friday, a special feeling can be observed in the entire country. On many street corners in the business areas, small stalls are set up and vendors sell lovely fresh flowers. Most people stop on their way home from work to buy flowers to brighten their homes and tables.

Since Israel is a Jewish country and most of the people who live there are Jewish, things can be done to celebrate Shabbat that are not possible elsewhere. Buses do not run. Government offices are closed. And the country comes almost to a standstill. Only workers in essential jobs, such as police officers and fire-fighters, work on Shabbat. The entire mood of the country is one of peace and contentment. The usual bustle of activity is gone. People stroll lazily along the street and in parks. Families share common experiences and troubles are forgotten.

Shabbat afternoon is a time for study and rest. Here, yeshiva students in Israel review their weekly lessons.

FOCUS:
ON THE IMAGES OF
SHABBAT

Shabbat was very important to Jews throughout the ages. Because it was so important, Jewish imagination built many stories and legends around it. Often the Jews thought of Shabbat as if it were a person. They called it a "queen" and said it was the "Queen of Days." They called it a "bride" because they were happy when it arrived, just as people are happy to see a bride. Poems were written about Shabbat. Songs were sung about it. One of the favorites is "Shalom Aleichem," which means "Peace to You:"

A Polish-Jewish woman blessing the Shabbat candles. Notice how the house has been cleaned for welcoming Shabbat. This painting is by Isidor Kaufmann.

I greet you, O messengers of the Lord,
Who is Ruler over rulers, the Holy One
—Whose name we must praise.

שָׁלוֹם עֲלֵיכֶם, מַלְאֲכֵי הַשָּׁרֵת,
מַלְאֲכֵי עֶלְיוֹן, מִמֶּלֶךְ מַלְכֵי
הַמְּלָכִים, הַקָּדוֹשׁ בָּרוּךְ הוּא.

Come in peace, and may you bring
To me and to all God's blessing of peace.

בּוֹאֲכֶם לְשָׁלוֹם, מַלְאֲכֵי הַשָּׁלוֹם,
מַלְאֲכֵי עֶלְיוֹן, מִמֶּלֶךְ מַלְכֵי
הַמְּלָכִים, הַקָּדוֹשׁ בָּרוּךְ הוּא.

HEBREW WORDS AND PHRASES

Below is a list of Hebrew words and phrases relating to Shabbat. See how many you can learn.

חַלָּה	**Challah**	Sabbath and holiday bread
זְמִירוֹת	**Zmirot**	Shabbat songs
חַזָּן	**Chazan**	Cantor
שַׁבָּת	**Shabbat**	The seventh day of the week, a day of rest
בֵּית־כְּנֶסֶת	**Bet Knesset**	Synagogue or temple
קִדּוּשׁ	**Kiddush**	Consecrating or making holy
בְּרָכָה	**B'racha**	A blessing
שַׁבָּת שָׁלוֹם	**Shabbat Shalom**	"A peaceful Sabbath!" (Shabbat greeting)
עֹנֶג שַׁבָּת	**Oneg Shabbat**	"Joy in the Sabbath" (social hour after Friday evening service)
סִדְרָה	**Sidrah**	Torah portion of the week
הַבְדָּלָה	**Havdalah**	"Separation" (prayer at end of Shabbath)
בְּשָׂמִים	**Besamim**	Spices
אֵלִיָּהוּ הַנָּבִיא	**Eliyahu Naavi**	Elijah the Prophet
סִידוּר	**Siddur**	Prayerbook
עֶרֶב שַׁבָּת	**Erev Shabbat**	Eve of the Sabbath
בִּרְכַּת הַנֵּרוֹת	**Birkat Hanerot**	Blessing of the candles
בִּרְכַּת הַמָּזוֹן	**Birkat Hamazon**	Blessing of the food (after Sabbath meal)

THE
TORAH CYCLE

Rabbi Akiva was a great rabbi and scholar who lived long ago. It was a very unhappy time. Rome ruled Judea, the country we now call Israel. The Romans did not allow scholars to teach the Torah. Rabbi Akiva did not obey the law. He taught the Torah. His students were afraid for him. "Do not teach the Torah," they begged. Rabbi Akiva did not listen. He told this story:

"Once a fish was swimming in a lake where fishermen were fishing. The fish was afraid and tried to swim away from the fishermen's hooks, but it could not. A hungry fox stood on the shore watching. 'If you come up on dry land, you will be safer,' said the fox. But the fish refused. 'If I am not safe in the water where I belong, I will not be safe on land,' it said.

"I am like that fish," said Rabbi Akiva. "If I am not safe teaching the Torah, which is my life, I will not be safe doing what is not natural to me.

—Tanhuma (Ki Tavo)

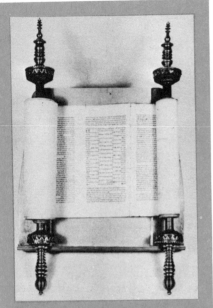

This is a Torah scroll. It is made of parchment and is written by hand. The Torah contains the first five books of the Bible.

It is the middle of Shabbat morning services at the temple. The rabbi steps up to the ark, pulls aside the curtain, and opens the door. Inside are Torah scrolls beautifully covered with special velvet coverings or encased in decorative silver containers. Each *Torah* is adorned with a silver breastplate and crown. The rabbi removes the Torah from the ark. An assistant from the congregation helps the rabbi remove the covering, the *tzitz* (breastplate), and the *keter* (crown). The rabbi unrolls the Torah and begins to read aloud in a special melody. In some congregations it is a cantor or a special Torah reader who reads from the Torah.

This ceremony is repeated every Shabbat morning in every temple and synagogue in the world. Jews everywhere cherish the Torah as a special symbol of Judaism. It is adorned with beautiful jewelry and kept in a beautiful ark. In many temples it is the custom to carry the Torah around the congregation before it is read. As it passes down the aisle, each person touches his or her fingers to the Torah and then kisses them. This symbolizes their love for the Torah.

WHAT IS THE TORAH?

The Torah is the first five books of the Bible, handwritten on a parchment scroll, and rolled around a roller. In Ashkenazic synagogues it is covered with a beautiful velvet covering. In Sephardic synagogues it is encased in a silver case.

A scene in a Spanish synagogue, from a very old Haggadah. In Sephardic synagogues, the reader's desk is always in the center of the synagogue. Note the people surrounding the reader's desk.

The Bible is made up of three sections or volumes. They are the Torah, the Prophets, and the Holy Writings. The first section, the Torah, has five books. They are named Genesis, Exodus, Leviticus, Numbers, and Deuteronomy. Sometimes the Torah is called the "Five Books of Moses" because many Jews believe that they were written by Moses at God's instruction. The Torah is made up of stories about Jewish heroes, history, and laws.

Sometimes the word Torah refers to the Jewish way of life, because all of Jewish life is based on the teachings in the Torah. Even the later development of Jewish law, the Talmud, is based on the laws of the Torah.

THE WEEKLY CYCLE OF TORAH READINGS

Each week a different portion of the Torah is read in the temple. The Torah is divided into sections. Each section is called a *Sidrah*. There are just enough Sidrot to complete the reading of the Torah in one year. At the end of the year, there is a festive celebration called Simchat Torah (you will learn more about this festival on page 82). As soon as the reading of all the portions is completed, it is begun all over again. The Torah is very precious to Jews, and there is always something new to learn. So we read the Torah from beginning to end each year and then start all over again.

Have you ever seen a Torah case like this one? The case opens down the center, and there is no velvet mantle for the holy scroll. This is the Oriental fashion.

A Torah crown (Keter Torah). The Keter Torah crowns the greatest asset of Judaism, the Torah.

שְׁמוֹת הַטְּעָמִים.
Names of the accents.

מֻנַּח זַרְקָא מֻנַּח סֶגּוֹל מֻנַּח
מֻנַּח רְבִיעִי מַהְפַּךְ פַּשְׁטָא זָקֵף
קָטֹן זָקֵף גָּדוֹל מֵרְכָא טִפְחָא מֻנַּח
אֶתְנַחְתָּא פָּזֵר תְּלִישָׁא־קְטַנָּה
תְּלִישָׁא־גְדוֹלָה קַדְמָא וְאַזְלָא
אַזְלָא־גֵרֵשׁ גֵּרְשַׁיִם דַּרְגָּא תְּבִיר
יְתִיב פְּסִיק ׀ סוֹף־פָּסוּק: שַׁלְשֶׁלֶת
קַרְנֵי־פָרָה מֵרְכָא־כְפוּלָה יֶרַח
בֶּן־יוֹמוֹ.

Along with the portion of the week, or Sidrah, there is another Biblical portion that is read. It is called the *Haftarah*. The Haftarah is not from the Torah, but from the Prophets. Usually the Haftarah has some relationship to the Torah Sidrah with which it is read.

The Torah is handwritten in a special script without periods, commas, or other punctuation. The words have no vowels. It must be chanted in a special way with special musical notes called trope. But even Jews who do not know how to read from the Torah like to participate in the reading. This is made possible by calling people to the pulpit to recite special blessings before and after each Torah reading. Those people are said to have an *Aliyah*. Having an Aliyah is a great honor. Boys and girls are given this honor on their Bar or Bat Mitzvah.

A special volume called a Tikkun is used to practice reading the Torah correctly. In the Tikkun the right-hand column includes vowel points and cantillation notes. In the left-hand column the same section is printed just as it appears in the Torah. The word Tikkun means "correction."

SOMETHING TO THINK ABOUT

The Torah scroll is usually beautifully adorned with velvet or silver coverings and decorated with silver jewelry. Why do you think this is so?

ON YOUR OWN

Attend a Shabbat morning service. Pay particular attention to the part of the service when the Torah is taken from the ark and read. Report to your class on what you experienced.

SHARING FEELINGS

The Torah is, and always has been, very precious to the Jewish people. Think of something that is very precious to you. Share your feelings about it with a friend.

HEBREW WORDS AND PHRASES

Below is a list of Hebrew words and phrases relating to the Torah. See how many you can learn.

תּוֹרָה	**Torah**	The Five Books of Moses
צִיץ	**Tzitz**	Torah breastplate
כֶּתֶר	**Keter**	Torah crown
סְדְרָה	**Sidrah**	Weekly Torah portion
סוֹפֵר	**Sofer**	Scribe who writes the Torah scroll by hand
הַפְטָרָה	**Haftarah**	Weekly portion from the Prophets
עֲלִיָּה	**Aliyah**	"Going up" to honor the Torah
פִּרְקֵי אָבוֹת	**Pirke Avot**	Ethics of the Fathers

A Torah scroll must be written in a very special way. It is written by someone who is specially trained. He is called a *sofer* (scribe). The Torah is written by hand in a special script. It is not written on paper but on parchment which is made from animal skins. The skins may be only from kosher animals. A special instrument is used to write the Torah. It is a feather pen or quill. The pieces of the scroll are sewn together with thread made from the sinew of kosher animals.

Writing a Torah scroll is long, hard, tedious work. There are very few people left who have the special skill and knowledge that is needed. A properly written scroll is rare. Not only are the words in it very precious, but the scroll itself is very precious.

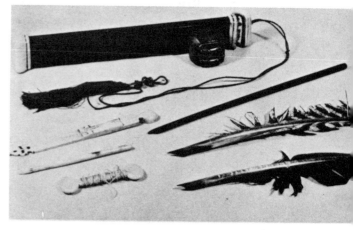

These tools are used in writing a Torah scroll. Here you see the inkwell, the reeds and their case, quills, and sinews (of kosher animals) for sewing parchment sheets together.

When a scribe (sofer) writes a Torah scroll, he rules guidelines with the blunt edge, and divides each parchment sheet into sections. Every Torah scroll must be entirely handwritten.

You know that the Torah is the first five books of the Bible, the Five Books of Moses. But the word Torah also means the "Jewish way of life." When we live according to the laws and customs of Judaism, it is said that we are living in the way of Torah. To live according to Torah, it is necessary to know what Torah is. Jews have always been encouraged to study Torah or the Jewish way of life.

Pirke Avot, or "Ethics of the Fathers," is an important book for Jews. It was written about two thousand years ago by the rabbis and wise sages of that time. Here are some of the things it has to say about the importance of studying Torah:

The world stands on three things: Torah, worship, and loving deeds.

Love your fellow creatures and draw them near to the Torah.

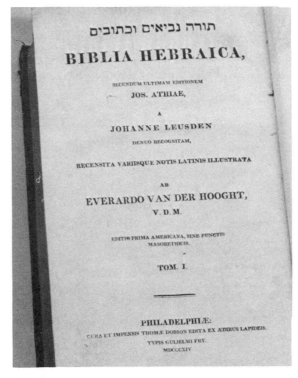

The first Hebrew Bible printed in America (Philadelphia, 1814).

Make your study of Torah a regular habit.

The more Torah, the more life.

Without Torah, there is no social order. Without social order, there is no Torah.

Turn the Torah over and over. It contains everything. Do not budge from the Torah. There is no better life than that.

45

LEARNING MORE ABOUT:
THE TORAH BLESSINGS

Before the Torah is read in the temple, special blessings are recited. People are called from the congregation to come up to the pulpit to recite the blessings. This is a very great honor. The people who are so honored are said to have an Aliyah. This means "calling up."

These are the blessings that are said before the Torah is read:

Let us praise God to whom all praise is due.
Praise God who is to be praised forever and ever.

בָּרְכוּ אֶת יְיָ הַמְבֹרָךְ.

בָּרוּךְ יְיָ הַמְבֹרָךְ לְעוֹלָם וָעֶד.

I praise God, who is Lord and Ruler over all, for having chosen us from among all peoples by giving to us the Torah. I praise God who has given to us the Torah.

בָּרוּךְ אַתָּה יְיָ, אֱלֹהֵינוּ מֶלֶךְ הָעוֹלָם, אֲשֶׁר בָּחַר בָּנוּ מִכָּל הָעַמִּים, וְנָתַן לָנוּ אֶת תּוֹרָתוֹ, בָּרוּךְ אַתָּה יְיָ נוֹתֵן הַתּוֹרָה.

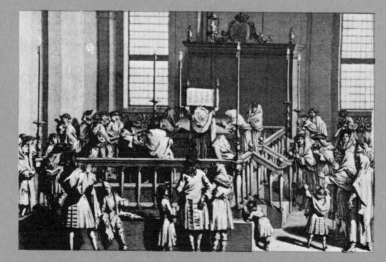

Bernard Picart's copper engraving of this synagogue scene shows the Hagbahah ceremony in the synagogue. The person lifting up the Torah scroll has opened it as wide as he can so that the congregation should be able to see as much text as possible.

After reading the Torah:

I praise God, who is Lord and Ruler over all, for giving to us a Torah of truth that we may live forever. I praise God who has given to us the Torah.

בָּרוּךְ אַתָּה יְיָ, אֱלֹהֵינוּ מֶלֶךְ הָעוֹלָם, אֲשֶׁר נָתַן לָנוּ תּוֹרַת אֱמֶת, וְחַיֵּי עוֹלָם נָטַע בְּתוֹכֵנוּ. בָּרוּךְ אַתָּה יְיָ נוֹתֵן הַתּוֹרָה.

UNIT III
THE JEWISH MONTH

Have you ever looked up at the moon in the night sky? If you have, then you must have noticed that it is not always the same. Sometimes it is large and round. Other times it is just a thin sliver. Our ancient ancestors noticed these changes in the size and shape of the moon. As they watched the sky they saw that the moon would start out one night as a barely visible sliver. Each night it would get larger until after many nights it was large and round. Then it would go back to being a sliver again. Each time the moon would start out barely visible, and after a number of days it would grow into a large, round ball.

Our ancestors watched the moon very carefully. Soon they realized something interesting. It took exactly 29 or 30 days from new moon to new moon. It never took less than 29 days. It never took more than 30 days. So accurate were their observations that they could tell in advance when the new moon would come. Soon they were measuring time from new moon to new moon. They called the period from new moon to new moon a *chodesh*, which means "new." We call it a "month." That was the beginning of the calendar. The calendar was very important to the ancient Jews. It helped them to count the years. It helped them to know when the holidays would arrive.

So important was the calendar to the ancient Jews that the beginning of each month was celebrated with special prayers and rituals. We still honor the new moon with special prayers.

In this unit you will learn about the Jewish calendar. You will learn how it developed and why it is important. You will also learn how the ancient Jews celebrated the new month and how we celebrate it in our time.

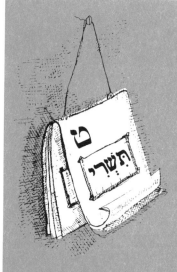

THE HEBREW CALENDAR

There is a season for everything and a time for every purpose under heaven. There is a time to be born and a time to die. There is a time to plant and a time to harvest. There is a time to kill and a time to heal. There is a time to destroy and a time to build. There is a time to cry and a time to laugh. There is a time to mourn and a time to dance. There is a time to cast away stones and a time to gather stones together. There is a time to embrace and a time not to embrace. There is a time to find and a time to lose. There is a time to keep and a time to throw away. There is a time to tear and a time to sew. There is a time to be quiet and a time to speak. There is a time to love and a time to hate. There is a time for war and a time for peace.

—Ecclesiastes 3:1–8

Have you ever wondered why Jewish holidays do not happen on the same day each year? Does it seem strange to you that Passover might begin on April 6 one year and on April 25 the next? Or that Rosh Hashana might come on September 18 one year and September 10 the following year? After all, Independence Day is always on July 4. And Thanksgiving always comes on the Thursday after the third Wednesday of November.

There is a very good and important reason for this. The Jewish holidays *do* come on the same dates each year. But they are not dates on the calendar we know, the calendar used in the United States, Canada, and Europe. There is another calendar that marks the Jewish year. It is completely different from the calendar with which we are familiar. The names of the months are different, and so are the names of the days. Even the numbers of the years are different.

In this chapter we will learn about the Jewish calendar *(luach)*. We will learn how it is different from our usual calendar, which we call the Gregorian calendar.

A page from a Jewish calendar.
Notice the variety of information.

A MOON CALENDAR

The calendar we use in everyday life is called the civil calendar, or sometimes the Gregarion calendar. It is a solar or sun, calendar, dividing days, months, and years according to the revolution of the earth around the sun and the rotation of the earth on its axis. It takes 24 hours for the earth to rotate on its axis. That is a day. It takes 365¼ days for the earth to circle the sun. A year is 365 days. Every fourth year there is an extra day added to make up for the extra ¼ day. That is a leap year.

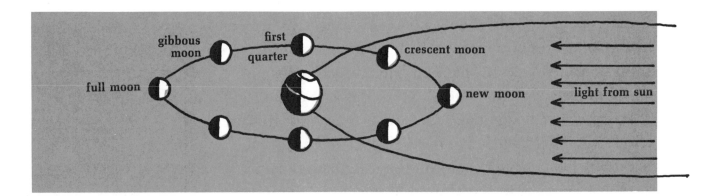

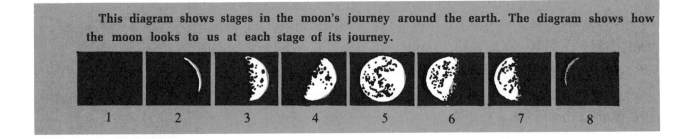

This diagram shows stages in the moon's journey around the earth. The diagram shows how the moon looks to us at each stage of its journey.

The Jewish calendar is a lunar, or moon calendar. It divides the time according to the cycles of the moon. You will understand what this means if you have ever noticed that the moon is not always the same. Some nights it is full and round. Other nights, you can hardly see it at all. If you watch closely, you will see that the moon starts out as a tiny sliver in the night sky. That is called a new moon. Each night, it gets a little bigger, until soon it is a large, round, yellow ball. That is called a full moon. The time period from the new moon to the new moon is called a moon cycle.

The ancient Jews noticed that it took about 29 or 30 days from new moon to new moon. They decided to measure time by these moon cycles. Jewish scholars developed a calendar using the moon cycles as the basic unit. They called the 29 or 30 days from new moon to new moon a *chodesh*, or month. They called twelve of these months a *shana*, or year.

But there was a problem. The sun year was 365 days long. The moon year of twelve months was 354 days long. It is the sun and its position in the sky that makes the seasons. When the sun is high in the sky, it is spring or summer. When the sun is low in the sky, it is autumn or winter. If the moon year is shorter than the sun year, the months could not keep up with the seasons. Soon, Passover would be in winter. Rosh Hashana would be in spring. Everything would be all mixed up.

A solution was found. In order to help the moon year catch up with the sun year, extra months were added to certain years. The years were called leap years. Every nineteen years there are seven leap years. They come every third, sixth, eighth, eleventh, fourteenth, seventeenth, and nineteenth Jewish year. This works out just right.

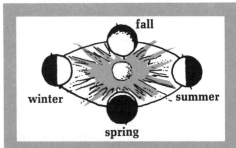

The position of the earth relevant to the sun gives us our seasons. Seasons are named here for the Northern Hemisphere. In the Southern Hemisphere the seasons are opposite.

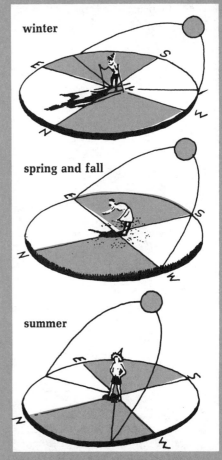

In winter, the sun follows a lower path across the sky than in the summer. In spring and fall, it follows a path in-between.

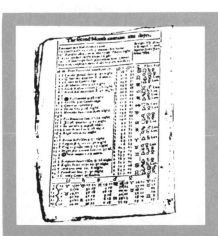

American Pilgrims drew their inspiration for a Thanksgiving Day from the festival of Sukkot in the Bible. They loved the Bible, even based their calendars on it. In this early American calendar of 1666, Pilgrims used the Hebrew names of the months.

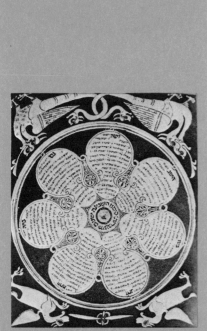

Before the invention of printing, the preparation of a calendar was a laborious undertaking. This calendar or luah of 5036 (1276) was found in a Bible manuscript.

If you wish to figure out the number of the Hebrew year, there is an easy formula. Subtract 1240 from the civil year. Then add 5000. The Hebrew year for 1981 would be:

$$
\begin{array}{r}
1981 \\
-1240 \\
\hline
741 \\
+5000 \\
\hline
5741
\end{array}
$$

That is the year if you are figuring it between January 1 and Rosh Hashana. If you are figuring it between Rosh Hashana and December 31, add one more year.

THE HEBREW DAYS

The Jewish week begins on Sunday. It ends on Saturday, or Shabbat. The names of the days are really numbers. They tell what day of the week it is. This is how the days are named in Hebrew:

> Sunday—Yom Rishon (The First Day)
> Monday—Yom Sheni (The Second Day)
> Tuesday—Yom Shlishi (The Third Day)
> Wednesday—Yom Revi'i (The Fourth Day)
> Thursday—Yom Chamishi (The Fifth Day)
> Friday—Yom Shishi (The Sixth Day)
> Saturday—Shabbat (The Sabbath)

Scholars believe that the seven-day week was a Jewish invention. The seven-day week with the last day, Shabbat, as a day of rest, was a very important Jewish gift to the world.

THE HEBREW MONTHS

The Hebrew months have names that are very different from the names of the months of the civil calendar.

54

Some of the names come from the Bible. But we do not know where many of the other names come from. We do know that they are very, very old. These are the names of the Hebrew months. Next to some are Jewish holidays that occur in those months.

תִּשְׁרֵי Tishri—Rosh Hashana, Yom Kippur, Sukkot

חֶשְׁוָן Cheshvan

כִּסְלֵו Kislev—Chanukah

טֵבֵת Tevet

שְׁבָט Shevat—Tu Bishvat

אֲדָר Adar—Purim

נִיסָן Nisan—Passover, Yom Hashoah

אִיָּר Iyar—Yom Haatzmaut, Lag B'Omer

סִיוָן Sivan—Shavuot

תַּמּוּז Tammuz

אָב Av—Tisha B'Av

אֱלוּל Elul

When there is a leap year, the extra month is added after Adar. It is called Adar Sheni, or Adar the second.

THE HEBREW YEAR

The Jewish year begins on Rosh Hashana. The number of the year is much higher than in the civil calendar. The years in the civil calendar are numbered from the beginning of Christianity. That was about two thousand years ago. The years in the Jewish calendar are numbered from the traditional date of the creation of the world. Thus it is sometimes called a creation calendar.

A design in the floor of a synagogue built at Bet Alpha in the sixth century C.E. There are signs of the zodiac, Jewish symbols, and inscriptions in Hebrew, Greek, and Aramaic.

This Hebrew Almanac, prepared by the Jewish astronomer Abraham Zacuto, was used by Christopher Columbus on his voyage to the New World. With it Columbus predicted an eclipse of the moon.

SOMETHING TO THINK ABOUT

The ancient Hebrews were farmers. It is very important for farmers to have a calendar. Why do you think this is so?

ON YOUR OWN

Get a Hebrew calendar. Look up the Hebrew dates for these important days:

> your birthday
> your next school vacation
> your mother's birthday
> your father's birthday
> your parents' anniversary

HEBREW WORDS AND PHRASES

Below is a list of Hebrew words and phrases relating to the Hebrew calendar. See how many you can learn.

לוּחַ	**Luach**	Hebrew calendar
חֹדֶשׁ	**Chodesh**	New (moon), a month
שָׁנָה	**Shana**	Year

LEARNING MORE ABOUT: TWO-DAY HOLIDAYS

Reform Jews celebrate the holidays of the Jewish year for one day, the same as the ancient Jews did in the time of the Bible. Orthodox and Conservative Jews, however, celebrate some of the holidays for two days. How did this come about?

Long ago the Jews lived in the Land of Israel. At that time they observed each holiday for only one day. They did not have written calendars the way we do today, but it was easy for them to figure out the dates of the holidays. All they had to do was look at the sky. If there was a new moon, they knew that a new month had started. Then they would count the days until the date of the next holiday.

But then powerful enemies conquered Israel. Many Jews were forced to leave their country and live all over the world. They continued to celebrate all their holidays as before even though they no longer lived in their homeland. But they did not know exactly when to celebrate the holidays. Since they did not know exactly when the new moon could be seen in Israel, they were not always certain when a new month had begun. In order to make sure that they did not celebrate the holidays on the wrong day, they started the custom of celebrating for two days.

The Jews who remained in Israel, of course, continued to celebrate the holidays for only one day. Since they always knew the right date because they were in Israel and could see the new moon, they didn't need a second day as a precaution against making mistakes. Nowadays this applies to us too. We have written calendars that tell us exactly when the new moon appears, even though we may not see it ourselves. Thus we always know when a new month begins, and we always know the dates of the holidays.

Since we no longer have the problem the two-day custom was meant to solve, it is really not needed anymore. That is why Reform Judaism decided to observe the holidays for only one day. Many Jews, however, enjoy the two-day custom as a warm reminder of our past history. What does your family do?

ROSH CHODESH

When God created the world, God made the sun and the moon equal. They were both the same size. They both gave equal light. But the moon was jealous. It did not want to be the same size as the sun. It wanted to be larger. It did not want to be as bright as the sun, it wanted to be brighter. The moon said to God, "The sun and I are the same size. Shouldn't one of us be larger? Shouldn't one of us be brighter?"

God was very angry at the moon for being jealous of the sun. "You are quite right," God said. "One of you should be larger and brighter. It will be the sun."

The moon was very unhappy. "Did I do such a terrible thing?" it asked. "I only spoke up once and yet you punished me so severely."

God was sorry. The moon would be smaller and dimmer than the sun. But God created the stars to brighten the sky at night when the moon shone.

—Midrash

The beginning of the new month is called *Rosh Chodesh*. It was a very important time for the ancient Jews. It is still an important time for many Jews who recite special prayers and blessings in its honor.

The Hebrew month begins on the evening of the new moon. In our time we know when that will be. We are able to calculate it scientifically. But in ancient times, it was much harder. The people knew around when to expect the new moon. But they did not know exactly. This is how it was decided when a new month had started. People would watch for the new moon. Whoever spotted it would report it to the *Sanhedrin*, the Jewish court and law-making body. As soon as two people reported a new moon, the Sanhedrin declared that the new month had begun.

The people were very happy to know that the new month had started. They welcomed it with prayers and feasting.

ROSH CHODESH IN ANCIENT TIMES

In ancient times, at the time of the First Temple *(Bet Hamikdesh)*, the beginning of the new month was celebrated with great festivity. The *shofar* was blown. People did not go to work. They came to Jerusalem. There they sacrificed a special new-month offering. Afterwards, a family feast was held. A special feature of the day was that women were released from all their chores. This was a reward for them because long before, when the Jews were wandering in the desert

A reconstruction of the Holy of Holies of the Temple in Jerusalem.

after leaving Egypt, the women had refused to contribute their jewelry to help build an idol.

After the First Temple was destroyed, many of these customs were no longer practiced. But other customs developed. Special prayers were said in honor of the new moon. One of the prayers was *Hallel.* It is a special prayer of praise to God that is recited only on holidays. But an exception is made for the new moon, when Half-Hallel is recited.

IN MODERN TIMES

The beginning of the new month is still celebrated with special prayers and customs in many modern temples. Usually the new moon is blessed following the Havdalah service on the Saturday night following its appearance. Often this lovely ceremony is held in the open air where the moon can be seen.

ROSH CHODESH PRAYERS AND BLESSINGS

You may want to learn some of the special prayers and blessings that are recited on Rosh Chodesh. One of them is Yehi Ratzon. It is a prayer for the new month:

May it be Your will, O God who is Lord and God of our ancestors, to renew for us this coming month for good and for blessing.

A reconstruction of the famous synagogue at Kfar Nahum (Capernaum).

An eighteenth-century European engraving showing the blessing of the new moon.

יְהִי רָצוֹן מִלְּפָנֶיךָ, יְיָ אֱלֹהֵינוּ וֵאלֹהֵי אֲבוֹתֵינוּ, שֶׁתְּחַדֵּשׁ עָלֵינוּ אֶת הַחֹדֶשׁ הַזֶּה, לְטוֹבָה וְלִבְרָכָה.

60

SOMETHING TO THINK ABOUT

What are some of the new customs that were introduced to celebrate Rosh Chodesh when the Jews no longer lived in Israel? How were they different from the customs before the Temple was destroyed? Can you think of any other Jewish customs that changed or were added over the years? Do you think that these changes helped the Jews to preserve Judaism in different times and different countries?

ON YOUR OWN

Become a moon-watcher. Each night look outside. Look at the moon. Is it a new moon? Is it a full moon? Is it in-between? Write your observations down next to the date. When you think you see a new moon, check a luach. Is it the beginning of a new Hebrew month?

HEBREW WORDS AND PHRASES

Below is a list of Hebrew words and phrases relating to Rosh Chodesh. See how many you can learn.

לוּחַ	**Luach**	Calendar
חֹדֶשׁ	**Chodesh**	Month
רֹאשׁ חֹדֶשׁ	**Rosh Chodesh**	Beginning of the month
תְּהִלִים	**Tehilim**	Psalms
סַנְהֶדְרִין	**Sanhedrin**	Court which ruled on matters of Jewish religious law
בֵּית־הַמִקְדָשׁ	**Bet Hamikdash**	The Holy Temple
שׁוֹפָר	**Shofar**	Ram's horn
הַלֵל	**Hallel**	Psalms of praise

Hallel means "praise." It is a name given to special prayers that are recited in the synagogue on the holidays of Sukkot, Passover, Shavuot, and Chanukah. On Rosh Chodesh only half of the prayer is said. In most synagogues in Israel, Hallel is also said on Yom Haatzmaut (Independence Day). The prayers come from the Book of Psalms (*Tehilim*) in the Bible. In ancient days the prayer was recited in the Temple on Passover eve.

The words of Hallel are very beautiful. This is part of the Hallel:

The opening words of the psalm in the Hallel prayer which begins, "When Israel left Egypt . . ."

This illustrated Hallel prayer shows the Children of Israel leaving Egypt. They are led by Moses and are passing through the gate of a medieval town from which the Egyptians are looking down.

HALLELUYAH.

O servants of God, praise the
Almighty.

Blessed be the Name of the Lord
From now and forever;
From the rising of the sun until it
sets,
The Lord's name is to be praised.

The Lord is above all nations.
The Lord's glory is above the
heavens.
Who is like the Lord our God,
Who looks down upon the heaven
and earth.

הַלְלוּיָהּ. הַלְלוּ עַבְדֵי יְיָ. הַלְלוּ
אֶת־שֵׁם יְיָ: יְהִי שֵׁם יְיָ מְבֹרָךְ.
מֵעַתָּה וְעַד־עוֹלָם: מִמִּזְרַח־
שֶׁמֶשׁ עַד־מְבוֹאוֹ. מְהֻלָּל שֵׁם
יְיָ:

רָם עַל־כָּל־גּוֹיִם יְיָ. עַל
הַשָּׁמַיִם כְּבוֹדוֹ: מִי כַּיְיָ אֱלֹהֵינוּ.
הַמַּגְבִּיהִי לָשָׁבֶת: הַמַּשְׁפִּילִי
לִרְאוֹת בַּשָּׁמַיִם וּבָאָרֶץ.

UNIT IV
THE JEWISH YEAR

Our ancient ancestors were farmers. They depended on their crops for food. Without a good harvest they would die of starvation. So the seasons of the harvest were very important to them. Many of the Jewish holidays were originally agricultural holidays.

But the Jewish holidays are all important for another reason. The Jews are a historical people. They have a long history. That history is not just part of their past. It is also part of our present. We remember the past of our people every time we celebrate a Jewish holiday. Most Jewish holidays have two meanings. They remind us of the agricultural festivals the Jews celebrated in ancient times when they were farmers. They also remind us of important events in Jewish history.

In this unit you will learn about all the Jewish holidays. Most of them are very, very old. They began long before history books were written. But some are very new. You will see that even some of the old holidays are celebrated in new ways.

Learning about the holidays of the Jewish year will help you to understand more about your Jewish heritage. You will learn why and how the holidays are celebrated and what makes being Jewish so very special.

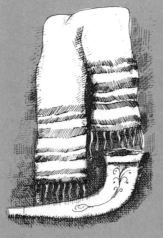

THE
HIGH HOLY DAYS

It is said that there are three books open in heaven on Rosh Hashana. In one are the names of the very good people. In the second are the names of the very bad people. In the third are the names of everyone in-between.

On Rosh Hashana, God writes the names of the very good in the Book of Life. The very bad, God writes in the Book of Death. But all those who are in-between are not written down on Rosh Hashana. God does not decide about them until Yom Kippur. Then God decides whether they are to be written in the Book of Life or the Book of Death

—Talmud

It is autumn. The long summer days have given way to shorter days and longer nights. The air is no longer as warm as it was. The heat of summer has changed to the cool breezes of fall. The leaves on the trees begin to change from bright green to brown and red. Soon, they will dry up and fall off the trees. And you have gone back to school after a long and leisurely vacation. But these are not the only changes that are taking place. There is an air of excitement in every Jewish home. Special preparations are being made. Soon the most sacred season of the Jewish year will arrive. Soon we will observe the High Holy Days.

The High Holy Days begin with *Rosh Hashana* and end with *Yom Kippur.* Between Rosh Hashana and Yom Kippur are ten days called *Aseret Y'may Teshuvah,* the Ten Days of Repentance. Rosh Hashana is the Jewish New Year. It is very different from the New Year that comes on January 1. On that New Year, people rejoice and have fun. But Rosh Hashana is a very serious day. On Rosh Hashana, Jews all over the world pray to God for a good year. They think about the kind of people they are and the kind of people they would like to be. They think of all the things they did in the year that has just ended. They remember their good deeds and their bad deeds. They make promises to themselves that in the year to come, they will be better people than in the past year.

This page of Slichot (repentance) prayers is from a nineteenth-century European High Holy Day prayerbook.

65

SLICHOT

The theme of the High Holy Days is forgiveness. If one person has harmed another during the year, he or she asks forgiveness. If a person has been harmed by another, he or she forgives. All Jews also ask forgiveness from God. They ask to be forgiven for any wrongs they did during the year.

The word *Slichot* means "forgiveness." It is also the name of a special prayer asking for forgiveness. Jews begin to put themselves in the proper frame of mind for the High Holy Days by reciting Slichot prayers before Rosh Hashana even begins. In some temples, the prayers are recited for the entire month of *Elul*, the month before the High Holy Days. In other temples, they are recited for a week, beginning on a Saturday night before Rosh Hashana.

The prayers are always recited late at night, after midnight or even later. In all temples where they are said, they help to set the solemn mood for the holiday season ahead.

ROSH HASHANA

Rosh Hashana means "the beginning of the year." The holiday also has other names. The names help to tell what the holiday means and why it is important.

YOM HADIN

One of the names for Rosh Hashana is *Yom Hadin*, "the day of judging." Jews believe that on this day they will be judged by God, who will decide whether they will live or die, whether they will have a good year or a sad year.

Israeli stamp with a Yom Kippur painting by the Jewish artist Maurycy Gottlieb.

Yom Kippur is the holiest day in the Jewish calendar. On this "Sabbath of Sabbaths," the entire day is spent in prayer and worship.

Jews also judge themselves on this day. They think about the things they did the year before. Were they as kind or considerate as they might have been? Were they as helpful? Were they as loving? Then they resolve to try to be better in the year to come. There is a tradition that we should always think of our deeds as evenly balanced on a scale between good and evil. Then each and every thing we do will tip the scales either to good or evil. Each action determines whether we are good people or bad people.

YOM HAZIKARON

Another name for Rosh Hashana is *Yom Hazikaron*, "the day of remembering." On Rosh Hashana we remember all that we are and all that we have done. We take stock of ourselves. We ask, "Am I happy with the kind of person I am? Have I always done the right thing? Can I do better?" We resolve to make the year ahead better than the year that was. We promise ourselves that we will try harder to be the kind of person we would like to be.

We also remember on Rosh Hashana that we belong to an ancient people with a long history. We feel a closeness to Jews all over the world. Some need our help. We resolve to help them. Others can help us and teach us many things. We resolve to learn from them. We also promise ourselves to learn more about our wonderful Jewish heritage with its rich traditions and wonderful way of looking at the world.

YOM TRUAH

Rosh Hashana is also called *Yom Truah*, "the day of blowing the shofar." The *shofar* is a ram's horn. In ancient days it was blown for many occasions. It was

Silver plate with artistically engraved shofar-blowing scene. Persian, nineteenth century.

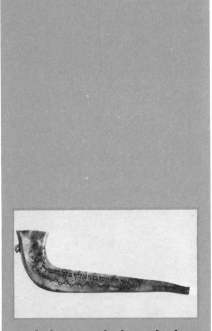

A shofar is made from the horn of a ram. The above is a German shofar from the year 1782.

The call of the shofar resounds in temples the world over on Rosh Hashana and Yom Kippur.

blown to announce a victory. It was blown just before Shabbat began. It was blown to announce the Jubilee year and each new month. In our time, it is blown only during Rosh Hashana services and at the end of Yom Kippur.

Before the shofar is blown, a special blessing is said:

I praise God, who is King and Ruler over all, who commanded us to hear the sound of the shofar.

בָּרוּךְ אַתָּה יְיָ, אֱלֹהֵינוּ מֶלֶךְ הָעוֹלָם, אֲשֶׁר
קִדְּשָׁנוּ בְּמִצְוֹתָיו וְצִוָּנוּ לִשְׁמוֹעַ קוֹל שׁוֹפָר.

ROSH HASHANA CUSTOMS

Rosh Hashana is observed each year on the first day of Tishri. It begins on the evening before with the blessing of the festival candles. Mother lights the candles and recites the blessings:

I praise God, who is Lord and Ruler over all,
for teaching us the commandment
of greeting this (Shabbat and) Festival by the lighting
  of candles.

בָּרוּךְ אַתָּה יְיָ אֱלֹהֵינוּ מֶלֶךְ הָעוֹלָם, אֲשֶׁר
קִדְּשָׁנוּ בְּמִצְוֹתָיו וְצִוָּנוּ לְהַדְלִיק נֵר שֶׁל (On
שַׁבָּת וְ) יוֹם טוֹב. Friday

I praise God, who is Lord and Ruler over all,
for keeping us well to reach this season.

בָּרוּךְ אַתָּה יְיָ, אֱלֹהֵינוּ מֶלֶךְ הָעוֹלָם, שֶׁהֶחֱיָנוּ
וְקִיְּמָנוּ וְהִגִּיעָנוּ לַזְּמַן הַזֶּה.

68

The entire family attends services in the temple. The services are conducted by the rabbi and chazan. Often, too, there is a choir that accompanies the chazan in the beautiful melodies and chants of the service. Many of these melodies are quite old. Others were written in more modern times. But all of them express the deep emotions that Jews feel at this special time.

The prayer service is read from a special prayerbook called a *Machzor* which contains the service for Rosh Hashana and Yom Kippur. The word Machzor comes from the Hebrew word *chazor*, which means "to repeat," because the service is repeated each year by Jews all over the world.

There are many special customs for Rosh Hashana. When we greet each other we say, *L'shana Tova Tikatevu*, "May you be written down for a good year." This refers to the belief that on Rosh Hashana, God writes down in a Book of Life what will happen to each person in the coming year. Sometimes this greeting is shortened to *Shana Tova*, "A good year," or "Happy New Year."

A very pleasant Rosh Hashana custom has to do with the foods we eat. Because we like to think of a sweet year, we eat sweet things. Before the meal, we dip apples and challah into honey. Everyone then wishes everyone else a good and sweet year *(Shana tova umetukah)*. The challah we eat on Rosh Hashana does not look like the usual braided challah we eat on Shabbat. Instead, it is a round, spiral loaf. When we eat it, we are saying that we hope that our lives will be round, full, and unending like the challah. Throughout the meal sweet things are eaten. Every family has its own traditions, but some of the foods for Rosh Hashana are tzimmis (made with carrots, meat, and honey),

The Bible says, "In the seventh month, on the first day of the month, shall be a solemn rest to you, a memorial proclaimed by a blast of shofrot . . ." (Leviticus 23:24).

A museum piece, this Rosh Hashana plate, used for challah, apples, and honey, was made in Delft, Holland, about 1700.

sweet noodle pudding, honey cake, and tayglach (pieces of dough cooked in honey).

An interesting old custom that is still observed by some Jews is that of *Tashlich.* A group of people walk to a park or out to the country where there is a stream of running water. There, they empty their pockets into the stream. They pray that just as the stream carries away the contents of their pockets, so will their sins be carried away.

THE TEN DAYS OF REPENTANCE

The ten days from Rosh Hashana until Yom Kippur are known as the Aseret Y'may Teshuvah (Ten Days of Repentance). It is a very serious and solemn time. Jews believe that it is during these days that they are judged by God. It is at this time that the fate of every person is decided. Is it any wonder that these days are filled with prayer and thoughtfulness? Each person thinks of the year to come. Each person hopes that it will be a good year—a year of peace, health, and contentment.

SHABBAT SHUVA

The Sabbath during the Ten Days of Repentance is called *Shabbat Shuva,* the Sabbath of Return. It takes its name from the Haftarah portion which is read that day. The portion begins with the word *Shuva.*

But the word shuva, or "return," has another meaning. It means return to God. It is a second chance, for those who believe that they have not been as good as they might be, to return to the right way.

Tashlich ceremony in Israel along the Mediterranean Sea.

The rabbi explains the meaning of the High Holy Days to a young worshipper.

70

YOM KIPPUR

Yom Kippur is the holiest and most important day of
the Jewish year. Jews all over the world fast on this day.
They do not eat any food or drink any liquid at all for
twenty-four hours. They also spend the entire day at
the temple in solemn prayer. Even Jews who do not
usually attend temple services the rest of the year
can be found at worship on Yom Kippur. It is on this
day, according to tradition, that the final verdict is
sealed. On this day will be decided the future of every
person in the world. Is it any wonder that it is such a
serious day?

KOL NIDRE NIGHT

On the evening before Yom Kippur Day, the entire
family gathers for the last meal before the fast. Since no
food or liquid will be allowed for twenty-four hours
after this meal, it is very carefully prepared. Light foods
are eaten and very little salt is used in the preparation
of the meal. Eating salt often makes people thirsty, and
this would not be a very good idea.

After the meal is over, the family goes to the temple.
The evening service for Yom Kippur is called *Kol
Nidre.* It takes its name from an ancient prayer by that
name. The cantor chants the prayer in a haunting
melody that is hundreds of years old. Many other
beautiful melodies are used for the prayers of the Yom
Kippur service. Most of the melodies are not like the
snappy, joyous melodies of the Shabbat service.
Instead, they are slow, thoughtful, and a bit sad, as
those who pray remember the many sad times in Jewish
history, and the sadness that still exists in our world
today.

Page with the Kol Nidre prayer,
from a Jewish-German Machzor
printed at Cracow, Poland, 1571.

שנה טובה

The High Holy Days are a time
for wishing our friends and relatives "a Shaua Tova, a happy and
healthy New Year." This elegant
greeting card expresses this senti-
ment.

YIZKOR

An important part of the Yom Kippur services is *Yizkor*, the memorial prayer for all those who have died and are remembered by close relatives in the congregation. Each person who has lost someone near and dear recites the prayer and fills in the name of the one who is being remembered. Another way that Jews remember dear relatives who have died is to light a memorial candle at home before leaving the house on Yom Kippur evening.

NEELAH

The service ends on Yom Kippur night with the recitation of the closing prayer called *Neelah*. Everyone is tired and hungry as the rabbi and cantor conclude the service. At the end of the service the shofar is blown. It is a long, loud blast. All return hopefully and happily to their homes to begin a new year. May it be a year of peace and contentment for all.

The cantor kneels before the open ark during the Neelah service.

This Yom Kippur Machzor, or prayerbook, was a mute witness to the cruel period of the Inquisition in Spain and Portugal. It was designed in this elongated shape for a special purpose. In case of a surprise "visit" by officers of the government, Marrano Jews (who pretended to be Christians but who practiced Judaism secretly) would drop the prayerbook into their wide sleeves and thus escape detection.

SOMETHING TO THINK ABOUT

Rosh Hashana, the Jewish New Year, is completely different from the New Year's Day that comes on January 1. It is celebrated differently. Its meaning is different. What are the differences between the two new years? Why do you think there are these differences?

SHARING

Make Shana Tova cards to send to your parents, relatives, and friends. Decorate them with crayons, paint, magic markers, bits of colored paper, tinsel, or anything else you can think of. Make sure each cards says "L'shana Tova Tikatevu" or "Shana Tova."

ON YOUR OWN

Make a list of all the things about yourself that you like. Then make a list of the things about yourself that you would like to change. Put a check next to those that you are able to change. Give yourself a time limit and work on those changes. Do not share your list with anyone else unless you really want to.

HEBREW WORDS AND PHRASES

Below is a list of Hebrew words and phrases relating to the High Holy Days. See how many you can learn.

יוֹם הַזִּכָּרוֹן	**Yom Hazikaron**	The Day of Remembering
יוֹם הַדִּין	**Yom Hadin**	The Day of Judgment
יוֹם תְּרוּעָה	**Yom Truah**	The Day of Blowing the Shofar
רֹאשׁ הַשָּׁנָה	**Rosh Hashana**	The Start of the New Year
לְשָׁנָה טוֹבָה תִּכָּתֵבוּ	**L'shana tova tikatevu**	"May you be written down for a good year" (Rosh Hashana greeting)
שׁוֹפָר	**Shofar**	Ram's horn
תִּשְׁרֵי	**Tishri**	The month of Rosh Hashana
מַחְזוֹר	**Machzor**	Prayerbook used on High Holy Days
עֲשֶׂרֶת יְמֵי תְּשׁוּבָה	**Aseret Y'may Teshuvah**	The Ten Days of Repentance—the ten-day period from Rosh Hashana to Yom Kippur
יוֹם כִּפּוּר	**Yom Kippur**	Day of Atonement
כָּל נִדְרֵי	**Kol Nidre**	"All the Vows" (famous prayer)
נְעִילָה	**Neelah**	Closing prayer on Yom Kippur
יִזְכּוֹר	**Yizkor**	Memorial prayer
שַׁבָּת שׁוּבָה	**Shabbat Shuva**	The Sabbath of Return
אֱלוּל	**Elul**	The month before Rosh Hashana and Yom Kippur
תַּשְׁלִיךְ	**Tashlich**	Ceremony of casting away one's sins

LEARNING MORE ABOUT:
THE HIGH HOLY DAYS IN THE SHTETL

The season of the High Holy Days was a very serious time in the shtetl. It began a whole month before at the beginning of the Hebrew month of Elul. People prepared very carefully for the New Year. They knew that at this time God would judge them. They tried to be especially good. They prayed harder than usual. They studied Torah each day. They were especially kind to their neighbors and friends. If they had done something wrong to someone else during the year, they made sure to apologize and ask forgiveness. The only ones who were joyful during this month were the children. They were happy because they did not have to go to school from the middle of the month of Elul until after Sukkot.

The day before Yom Kippur was a very busy one in the shtetl. Since Yom Kippur is a fast-day, the people believed that it was a mitzvah to eat heartily the day before. So all sorts of delicious foods were prepared.

Services were held in the synagogue on Yom Kippur evening and all during the day of Yom Kippur. The streets were very quiet during those times. No one was out. Everyone was in the synagogue praying. When the Yom Kippur service was over on Yom Kippur day, the people went home. But they did not have time for a large meal after their fast. They had a snack and then immediately began to build the sukkah which they would need to celebrate the next holiday.

Israeli stamp with drawing of the synagogue of Rabbi Israel Baal Shem Tov. Most synagogues in the Polish villages were built of wood.

On the Sunday before Rosh Hashana, Slichot services began. The services were held in the middle of the night before the sun rises. To make sure that no one would miss these important prayers, a special messenger went around to each house. He knocked on the door with a wooden hammer. The loud noise awakened the people. Sleepily they dressed and went to the synagogue. Slichot services were held each night until Rosh Hashana.

On the eve of Rosh Hashana everyone attended services. After services they returned to their homes for a festive meal. On the table was a plate of honey. The honey was spread on challah as a symbol of a sweet year.

The next day, services were again held in the synagogue. They began early in the morning and did not end until mid-afternoon. As part of the service the shofar was blown. Then there was lunch, after which most of the people of the town walked to a stream for the Tashlich ceremony. The second day, services were held again at the synagogue. Everyone was very solemn and serious during the entire two days of Rosh Hashana. But there was also time for enjoying friends and family as the greeting "L'shana Tova Tikatevu" was exchanged.

Tashlich ceremony in the shtetl.

SUKKOT AND SIMCHAT TORAH

There are four kinds of people in the world. They are like the four kinds of plants that make up the lulav and the etrog. There are those people who study the Torah and do good deeds. They are like the etrog, which smells good and tastes good. There are those people who study the Torah but do not do good deeds. They are like the branch of the palm tree, which has fruit that is good to eat but no pleasant smell. There are those people who do good deeds but do not study the Torah. They are like the branch of the myrtle tree, which has a pleasant smell but does not have fruit that is good to eat. Then there are those people who neither study Torah nor do good deeds. They are like the branches of the willow tree, which does not have a pleasant smell and does not bear fruit that tastes good.

—Pesikta de Rab Kahana (Midrash)

Following closely on the heels of Rosh Hashana and Yom Kippur is the joyous holiday of Sukkot, which takes place on the fifteenth day of Tishri. Not long after, on the twenty-third of Tishri, comes the holiday of Simchat Torah. Among Orthodox and Conservative Jews, Simchat Torah is considered to be the final day of a nine-day holiday that begins on Sukkot. Reform Jews in Israel consider Shemini Atzeret the eighth and final day of Sukkot. You will learn more about Simchat Torah later in this chapter.

THE SUKKAH

The most important symbol of Sukkot is the *sukkah* itself. The sukkah is a small hut or booth. Often it is made of boards nailed together. Sometimes it is prefabricated and kept from year to year. It is just sturdy enough to be used for a few days and offers no real protection against wind or rain. There is no permanent roof. Instead, leafy branches are thrown loosely over the top. From inside the sky can be seen.

The sukkah is a reminder of the temporary shelters used by the Jews in ancient times. Just as those shelters did not protect against the elements, so too must the sukkah be built so that it does not protect against the elements.

In our time most sukkot are built in the courtyards of temples. The worshippers stop in after services to eat some refreshments and recite the special blessings that are said in the sukkah. But many families have their own sukkah. They build it themselves and have all their meals there for the entire festival. Some Jews even sleep in the sukkah.

An Arab family gathering their harvest in the same manner as their ancestors, thousands of years ago. In the foreground is a sukkah built of branches and leaves to provide shade from the hot afternoon sun.

It is considered a mitzvah to eat at least something in the sukkah and to recite the sukkah blessings. These are the blessings that are said before beginning a meal in the sukkah:

I praise God, who is Lord and Ruler over all,
for teaching us the commandment of dwelling in the
*   sukkah.*

בָּרוּךְ אַתָּה יְיָ אֱלֹהֵינוּ מֶלֶךְ הָעוֹלָם, אֲשֶׁר
קִדְּשָׁנוּ בְּמִצְוֹתָיו וְצִוָּנוּ לֵישֵׁב בַּסֻּכָּה.

I praise God, who is Lord and Ruler over all,
for keeping us well to reach this season.

בָּרוּךְ אַתָּה יְיָ, אֱלֹהֵינוּ מֶלֶךְ הָעוֹלָם, שֶׁהֶחֱיָנוּ
וְקִיְּמָנוּ וְהִגִּיעָנוּ לַזְּמַן הַזֶּה.

THE SUKKAH AS A HISTORICAL SYMBOL

The Jews are a historical people. This means that their history and what happened to them in the past is very important to them. Each holiday symbol is seen as it relates to an important event in the history of the Jews.

The sukkah was a temporary shelter that the Jews used long, long ago when they were farmers. They built sukkot during the harvest season so that they would not have to leave their crops unguarded overnight. The festival of Sukkot took place during the harvest season. The temporary shelters called sukkot were very important because they helped the farmers to take care of their crops and reap a good harvest.

Everybody participates in building the sukkah.

But the Jews of long ago wanted the sukkah to have a historical meaning too. That way they could feel close to their past and their heritage. So on Sukkot they also remembered a very important event in ancient Jewish history. They remembered the Exodus from Egypt. That is when the Jews were freed from slavery. You will learn more about it when you read the chapter on Passover. The Jews of long ago said that the sukkah reminded them of the temporary shelters that their ancestors built when they were traveling in the desert after leaving Egypt. So the holiday of Sukkot came to have two meanings. It is a harvest festival. And it is also a reminder of that important time in Jewish history when the Jews were wanderers in the desert after leaving Egypt.

BUILDING A SUKKAH

Building a sukkah is not really difficult, and any family that has some space in its yard and wishes to do so can have its own sukkah. Basically, every sukkah has four walls, a straw roof, and a doorway or opening. The walls can be made of any one of a number of different materials. They can be canvas, wooden boards, or even chicken wire covered with leaves. The roof may be made of straw, corn husks, or branches of trees. It is traditional to leave an opening so that the sky may be seen. Usually the inside of the sukkah is decorated with pictures, daisy chains, and fruit hung from the walls and roof. The fruit symbolizes the bounty of the harvest. The building of the sukkah is usually begun when the family returns from the temple on Yom Kippur night.

Young Chasidim in Israel erecting a sukkah.

The fragrance and color of Indian corn, fruits, and vegetables remind us of the beauty of the harvest. Young and old help decorate the sukkah.

THE LULAV AND THE ETROG

Another very important symbol of Sukkot is the *lulav* and the *etrog*. These are made up of parts of four trees and symbolize the harvest. The parts of the four trees which are used are the etrog (the fruit of the citron tree), a branch of the palm tree, a branch of the *aravah* (willow) tree, and a branch of the *hadas* (myrtle) tree. The three branches are tied together in a special way and held in one hand while the etrog is held in the other. The palm branch with the myrtle and willow attached is called a lulav. A special blessing is recited over the etrog and the lulav. The blessing is:

בָּרוּךְ אַתָּה יְיָ, אֱלֹהֵינוּ מֶלֶךְ הָעוֹלָם, אֲשֶׁר קִדְּשָׁנוּ בְּמִצְוֹתָיו וְצִוָּנוּ עַל נְטִילַת לוּלָב.

I praise God, who is Lord and Ruler over all, for commanding us to bless the lulav.

In many temples there is also a procession led by the rabbi and the cantor carrying the etrog and lulav. A special hymn called Hoshanna is sung.

SHEMINI ATZERET

For Orthodox and Conservative Jews, Sukkot is the longest holiday of the year, lasting nine days. Because of the custom explained in the chapter on the Hebrew calendar, the Sukkot holiday begins as a two-day festival. After this come the five intermediate days of Sukkot, known in Hebrew as *Chol Hamoed*. These are observed as half-holidays. People are allowed to work and perform their normal activities, but the

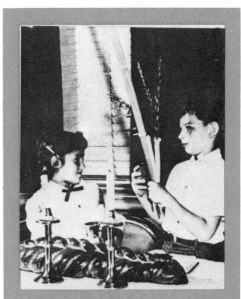

A Sukkot table with a giant challah and candlesticks. The boy is about to recite the blessing over the lulav and etrog.

The four kinds of growing things: etrog, lulav, hadas, and aravah.

Sukkot at the Western Wall in Jerusalem, Israel.

An early paper flag for Simhat Torah shows King David kneeling. The text reads; "David rejoiced on Simhat Torah."

lulav and etrog are used in the daily services, except on Shabbat, and it is customary to eat in the sukkah. Next comes the eighth day of Sukkot, which is called Shemini Atzeret.

Shemini Atzeret is really a separate festival and has its own special customs. As on Yom Kippur, Yizkor, the memorial prayer, is said for close relatives who have died. An interesting feature of the service is the reciting of the ancient prayer for rain. This prayer is called *Geshem,* which means "rain."

Our ancestors were farmers. Rain was very important to them. Without rain their crops would fail. There would be no crops to harvest and no food for the rest of the year. So they prayed to God to provide rain.

For many hundreds of years the Jews did not live in their homeland, Israel. They did not have a land of their own and they were not farmers. But they continued to recite the prayer for rain as a way of remembering their ancient heritage. They knew that someday they would again be in their own land.

Now that Israel is once more a Jewish homeland, the prayer for rain takes on added importance. Once more Jews are farmers and rain is necessary to make their crops grow.

SIMCHAT TORAH

Following the method of counting mentioned in the preceding section, the holiday of Simchat Torah, which comes right after Shemini Atzeret, is really the ninth day of Sukkot. The name *Simchat Torah* means "rejoicing with the Torah." It is a very happy holiday and is celebrated with much gaiety and festivity.

You remember reading about the cycle of Torah

82

readings on page 41. There you learned that the Torah is divided into as many portions, or Sidrot, as it takes to read one portion, or Sidrah, each week. The last Sidrah is read on Simchat Torah. Then the Torah is begun all over again from the very first chapter, the Chapter Bereshit, or "In the Beginning."

To the Jews, the Torah never ends. There is always something new to learn. So on the same day that the last chapter is read, they begin again with the first chapter. This is done with special ceremonies and a great deal of rejoicing. The Torah is very precious, and all Jews want to show how happy they are that they can read the Torah over and over each year and continue learning from it.

The first sentence in the Book of Genesis: "In the beginning God created the heaven and the earth." From a Bible printed in Prague in 1518. Only two copies of this book are in existence.

On Simchat Torah, the Holy Scrolls are carried around the temple in a gay procession. Children, holding Simchat Torah flags aloft, follow the adults as they circle the temple.

The temple service on Simchat Torah is the most joyous of the entire year. In many temples, the members of the congregation dance and sing as they carry the Torahs around the sanctuary in a happy procession. Children follow behind carrying flags topped with apples and sometimes with candles. The procession, known as *hakafot,* circles the temple seven times. Each time different people carry the scrolls until everyone over the age of thirteen has had a chance to carry a Torah.

In order to give even young children a chance to participate in the service, all the children under the age of thirteen are called to the Torah. A large tallit is held over their heads as together they chant the Torah blessings.

When the Torah reading has been completed and the service is ended, refreshments are served. This ends the fall holiday season which began so solemnly with the observance of Rosh Hashana.

A happy hakafot procession with flags and Torah.

SOMETHING TO THINK ABOUT

Sukkot was the holiday on which the Jews gave thanks to God for a bountiful harvest. Thanksgiving Day was the holiday on which the early settlers in America gave thanks to God for a bountiful harvest. How are the two holidays the same? How are they different? How is each holiday celebrated? What do these holidays mean?

SHARING

Make a list of all the things for which you are thankful. Share your list with your classmates.

HEBREW WORDS AND PHRASES

Below is a list of Hebrew words and phrases relating to Sukkot. See how many you can learn.

סוּכּוֹת	**Sukkot**	Festival of Booths
לוּלָב	**Lulav**	Palm leaf, willow branch, and myrtle branch bound together
אֶתְרוֹג	**Etrog**	Citron fruit
שְׁמִינִי עֲצֶרֶת	**Shemini Atzeret**	Eighth day of Sukkot
סוּכָּה	**Sukkah**	A booth made out of branches
עֲרָבָה	**Aravah**	Willow branch
הֲדַס	**Hadas**	Myrtle branch
שִׂמְחַת־תּוֹרָה	**Simchat Torah**	"Rejoicing with the Torah"
הַקָּפוֹת	**Hakafot**	Processions with the Torah
הוֹשַׁעְנָא	**Hoshanna**	A special hymn

The days before Sukkot were very busy ones in the shtetl. Every home had its own sukkah, and everyone who was able to, helped in building it. Young and old became master-builders, gathering slabs of wood, hammering boards together, and constructing a hut that would last for the eight days of the holiday. The sukkot were very simply built. Usually, it was necessary to build only two walls since the sukkah rested against the house, which formed one wall. The fourth side was left unbuilt and served as the entranceway. Once the holiday started, all the meals were eaten in the sukkah.

The lulav and etrog were an important part of the celebration in the shtetl. Everyone who could afford to buy a lulav and etrog did. But since they had to be imported and were very expensive, and most of the Jews in the shtetl were very poor, only a few very rich people could own their own. Sometimes a few families would get together and "chip in" to buy an etrog and lulav which they would all use. Those who could not afford to do even this used one of the few etrogim that belonged to the community. These were passed around so that each person could fulfill the mitzvah of reciting the blessing.

A father and son in Chasidic costume recite the blessing over the lulav and etrog.

Simchat Torah was an especially joyous time in the shtetl. On the evening of the holiday, after the prayers had been recited, there was a Torah procession. The men carried the Torah scrolls around the synagogue as they sang happy songs. From time to time they would stop, form a circle, and dance. The young children followed, carrying flags, on top of which were apples. Each apple had a hole into which was placed a candle. Even the women, who were not usually permitted to come into the men's sanctuary, were allowed to come down for this occasion to kiss the Torah as it was carried by.

The service on Simchat Torah morning was very long. Each man in the congregation was called up to the Torah to recite the blessings. The last section of the Torah was read over and over again to give each one a turn. This took a very long time. As on the night before, there was dancing and singing, and merrymaking. Simchat Torah was one of the happiest times of all in the shtetl.

CHANUKAH

Judah and his brothers said, "Now that our enemies are defeated, let us purify and rededicate the Temple. So the entire army gathered and went up to Mount Zion. There they saw that the Temple was uncared for and deserted. The altar was dirty. The Temple gates were burned up. Weeds grew as high as trees in the courtyard. The priests' rooms were torn down.

The soldiers were very sad to see their holy Temple in such a terrible condition. They tore their clothes and cried. They blew sad blasts on their shofars and they prayed to God. Judah appointed priests to clean and restore the Temple. He stationed soldiers outside to stand guard. Soon the Temple was clean and beautiful again. It was a fit place in which to offer sacrifices and to worship God.

All the people were overjoyed. Judah and his brothers and all who were there decided that each year on the twenty-fifth day of the month of Kislev, for eight days, there would be a joyous holiday to celebrate the rededication of the Temple.

—I Maccabees, chap. 4

Most Jewish holidays are described in the Bible. They go back many, many years to ancient times. They began long before people began to write history books. But *Chanukah* is different. It is one of the few holidays that celebrates an actual historical event, one that is told about in history books. (The new holidays of Yom Hashoah and Yom Haatzmaut are the only two others. You will read about them further on.) The other Jewish holidays are very, very old. We do not know when they began. But Chanukah is fairly new as Jewish history goes, and we know the year when it began. It began in 165 B.C.E., about two thousand years ago. Does that seem like a very long time ago to you? It is. But when you consider that the Jewish people have been around for about four thousand years, two thousand years is not such a long time, historically speaking.

Let us go back into history and trace the events that gave us this wonderful, happy holiday.

THE HISTORY OF CHANUKAH

Let us trace the interesting historical background of the holiday of Chanukah. In order to do so we will have to go back about two hundred years before the first Chanukah. We will have to go back to the mighty King Alexander of Greece. About 336 B.C.E. Alexander became ruler of most of the known world. He did this by conquering all the nations around the Mediterranean Sea. Israel was one of the nations in Alexander's empire.

Alexander the Great, king of Macedonia (336–323 B.C.E.), figures prominently in Jewish legend.

Israeli stamp featuring a coin from the period of the Maccabees.

Marble bust of Antiochus III. This bust was discovered in Italy and was acquired by Napoleon.

When Alexander died, his generals divided his great empire into four countries. Syria was one of these countries and Egypt was another. Judea, which we now call Israel, was between these two countries. Syria and Egypt were enemies. There are many wars between them. Judea was caught in the middle. Each needed Judea in order to reach the other. As the two nations battled, Judea would become first a part of Syria, then a part of Egypt, then a part of Syria again, and so on.

In 175 B.C.E. Antiochus became the king of Syria. Judea was then owned by Syria. Antiochus wanted to make sure that Judea would continue to be a part of Syria. He thought he could do this by making the Jews just like the Syrians. He thought that if he could get the Jews to behave like Syrians, think like Syrians, and believe as the Syrians believed, they would be loyal to Syria. Then, if there was another war with Egypt, the Jews would fight on the Syrian side, and Egypt would not be able to conquer Judea. Antiochus encouraged the Jews to assimilate. That means, to become just like the Syrians. He introduced the Greek language spoken by the Syrians. He encouraged Jews to participate in the Greek-style sports that were popular in Syria. He urged the Jews to give their children Greek names and study Greek books as the Syrians did. He even sent Greek idols that he worshipped to be placed in the Holy Temple.

But these methods did not work. Some of the Jews did become like the Syrians. They adopted the same Greek ways that the Syrians followed. There is a name for this. We call it becoming "Hellenized." But most Jews did not become Hellenized. They loved the Jewish way of life. They loved the Hebrew language. And they were loyal Jews who followed their religion.

Antiochus soon realized that the Jews would not willingly become Hellenized. He decided to force them to assimilate. He made laws that no Jewish religious practices could be observed. He placed idols in the Temple and in the marketplaces of all the towns. Then he sent his soldiers throughout the country to force the Jews to bow down to the idols and worship them.

One day the soldiers came to the small town of Modin. They set up an idol in the center of town and forced many of the people to bow down before it. Mattathias *(Matityahu)* lived in Modin. He was a loyal Jew. He watched sadly as others were forced to bow to the idol. But when his turn came, he refused to bow. He raised his sword and killed the Syrian soldier. Then he called to the Jews, "Let whoever is loyal to God come with me." Then Mattathias, his five sons, and all those who chose to follow fled to the hills surrounding the city. There they decided that they would fight the king. Judah, one of the sons of Mattathias, would be their leader, and they would fight for the right to worship God in their own way and follow the customs and rituals of their religion.

Copper half-shekel of Simon Maccabeus.

An enameled picture of Judah Maccabee. It was painted in the 15th century by a French painter.

A Greek soldier under attack. He wears a metal helmet and breastplate. This painting was found on an ancient stone coffin.

For three years, Judah the Maccabee (*Yehuda Ha-Maccabee*) led his followers in guerilla warfare. Those who study military strategy have said that his leadership as a general was brilliant. Even today, soldiers can use many of the techniques used by Judah Maccabee and his followers when they fought the Syrians in the hills of Judea. And they won. The Jews won their independence and the right to worship God in their own way.

As soon as the war was over, Judah gathered his soldiers and they went to Jerusalem (*Yerushalayim*) to clean the idols out of the Temple and restore it as the beautiful shrine it had been. Then they decided to hold a festival of rededication that we call Chanukah.

This drawing shows Judah Maccabee and his soldiers fighting for the freedom of Jerusalem.

THE MIRACLE OF THE LIGHTS

The rabbis of the Talmud did not like the idea of a holiday to celebrate a military victory. They thought that every holiday should be celebrated as a religious holiday. They gave another meaning to the holiday. They said it was celebrated because God performed a miracle in the Temple when it was being rededicated. They called the holiday the Festival of Lights. This is the story about it in the Talmud:

When the Syrians went into the Temple, they destroyed all the pure oil that is used to light the eternal light. The Maccabees won a victory and came to the Temple to clean and rededicate it. They looked for oil so that they could light the eternal light. But they could find only one small jar of oil, enough to burn for one day. A miracle happened and there was light from it for eight days. The next year they extended the holiday to eight days.

—Megillat Taanit

CHANUKAH CUSTOMS

Chanukah is a very happy holiday. It is a great favorite, especially among children, and it is celebrated with great joy. Many special customs have developed over the years to make the holiday more meaningful and more fun.

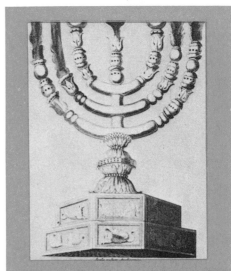

A picture of the seven-branched Temple menorah. It was in a menorah such as this that the miracle of the holy oil was said to have occurred.

A group of American soldiers conduct Chanukah services around a huge electric menorah

LIGHTING CHANUKAH CANDLES

Chanukah candles are lit at home on all eight nights of Chanukah. Many temples and religious schools also have public candle-lighting ceremonies for the whole community. On the first night one candle is lit. On the second night two candles, and so on. The candles are placed in a special menorah, or candelabra, called a *chanukia*. The chanukia has holders for nine candles, one for each day and a ninth called a *shamash*. The word shamash means "servant." The shamash, or servant candle, is lit first. Then it is used to light the other candles. There are two special blessings that are said or sung as the candles are lit. They are:

*I praise God, who is Lord and Ruler over all,
for teaching us the commandment of lighting the
   Chanukah candle.*

בָּרוּךְ אַתָּה יְיָ, אֱלֹהֵינוּ מֶלֶךְ הָעוֹלָם, אֲשֶׁר קִדְּשָׁנוּ בְּמִצְוֹתָיו וְצִוָּנוּ לְהַדְלִיק נֵר שֶׁל חֲנֻכָּה.

*I praise God, who is Lord and Ruler over all,
for doing wonders in days of old, at this season.*

בָּרוּךְ אַתָּה יְיָ, אֱלֹהֵינוּ מֶלֶךְ הָעוֹלָם שֶׁעָשָׂה נִסִּים לַאֲבוֹתֵינוּ, בַּיָּמִים הָהֵם בַּזְּמַן הַזֶּה.

A modern-day reenactment of the Chanukah story.

The chanukia reflects the shape of the moriah plant, which is found in Israel.

On the first night of Chanukah we add this blessing:

I praise God, who is Lord and Ruler over all,
for keeping us well to reach this season.

בָּרוּךְ אַתָּה יְיָ, אֱלֹהֵינוּ מֶלֶךְ הָעוֹלָם, שֶׁהֶחֱיָנוּ
וְקִיְּמָנוּ וְהִגִּיעָנוּ לַזְּמַן הַזֶּה.

    After the candles are lit, songs are sung and gifts
exchanged. The chanukia is then placed on the window
so that all who pass can be cheered by the light of the
Chanukah candles. Sometimes an electric menorah is
placed in the window.

A picture of a High Priest pouring oil into the Temple menorah.
From a 13th century French manuscript written by Benjamin, the Scribe.

THE DREIDEL

A favorite game that is played on Chanukah is that of dreidel *(s'veevon)*. The dreidel is a four-sided top with the Hebrew letters *Nun, Gimel, Hay,* and *Shin* on both sides. The letters stand for the Hebrew phrase:

A great miracle happened there.

Each letter is given a special value, such as "take all," "lose all," "take half," and so on. The dreidel is spun by each player, who then does whatever the letter stands for that the dreidel falls on. It is great fun, although no one really knows why this game is especially played on Chanukah.

CHANUKAH FOODS

One of the most enjoyable customs of Chanukah is the eating of special foods. Since the holiday is associated with oil (remember the jar of oil that burned eight days), all sorts of foods fried in oil are eaten on Chanukah. Two foods especially have become traditional, one in the United States, and one in Israel.

The food most usually eaten in celebration of Chanukah in our country is latkes *(l'vee-vot),* potato pancakes.

In Israel the favorite food for Chanukah is doughnuts fried in oil. The Israelis call these delicious cakes *sufganiot.* The Israelis also eat potato pancakes. They call them *l'veevot.*

Dreidels are made in many shapes. This one, of wood, is an Eastern European nineteenth-century dreidel.

Chanukah is not complete without a jolly dreidel-spinning game. Nun, gimel, hay, and shin are the Hebrew letters on the Chanukah top. They stand for Nes Gadol Hayah Sham, "a great miracle happened there."

CHANUKAH GIFTS

A Chanukah custom that has developed in recent years is that of exchanging gifts on Chanukah. Long ago it was the custom to give a few coins to each child after the candles were lit. This was called giving Chanukah "gelt," or Chanukah money. But in our time the exchanging of gifts has become customary. In some families each child is given a small gift each night after the candles are lit.

CHANUKAH AND CHRISTMAS

The Jewish holiday of Chanukah and the Christian holiday of Christmas both come in the winter, often very close to each other in time. This has led many people, both Christians and Jews, to think that there is some connection between the two holidays. Some people have even referred to Chanukah as the Jewish Christmas. But this is not so. The two holidays are not related in any way. They are not at all like each other.

Christmas is a very sacred day to the Christians. It is celebrated with services and special ceremonies. It is one of the holiest days in the Christian year. Chanukah, on the other hand, does not have the same degree of religious significance, and it is not even mentioned in the Bible.

Nonetheless, Chanukah means something very special to Jews. It stands for their desire to remain Jews no matter how hard it is. It reminds them that sometimes you have to sacrifice for your beliefs. Chanukah commemorates the first time that any religious group fought for the right to observe its religion. Many others have fought that fight since. But the Jews were the first. It was another great lesson they taught the world.

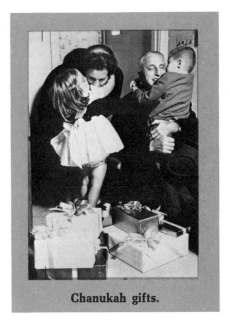

Chanukah gifts.

SOMETHING TO THINK ABOUT

Chanukah is called the Feast of Rededication because the Temple in Jerusalem was rededicated by the Maccabees after their victory. What does the word "dedication" mean? Have you ever "dedicated" or "rededicated" yourself to something? Is there anything you would like to "dedicate" yourself to?

SHARING

Have a Chanukah party. Invite the members of your class. Make l'veevot and sufganiot. Exchange Chanukah gifts. Make sure to light the Chanukah candles and recite the blessings. Sing Chanukah songs. Have a wonderful time.

HEBREW WORDS AND PHRASES

Below is a list of Hebrew words and phrases relating to Chanukah. See how many you can learn.

Hebrew	Transliteration	Meaning
חֲנוּכָּה	Chanukah	Dedication
סְבִיבוֹן	S'veevon	Spinning top (dreidel in Yiddish)
לְבִיבוֹת	L'veevot	Potato pancakes (latkes in Yiddish)
כִּסְלֵו	Kislev	Ninth month of Hebrew calendar
שַׁמָּשׁ	Shamash	"Servant" candle
יְהוּדָה הַמַּכַּבִּי	Yehuda Ha-Maccabee	Judah Maccabee, the general who defeated the Syrians
חַנָּה	Channah	Heroic mother who refused to worship Syrian idols
מַתִּתְיָהוּ	Matityahu	Mattathias
יְרוּשָׁלַיִם	Yerushalayim	Jerusalem
חֲנוּכָּה	Chanukia	Chanukah menorah
נֵס גָּדוֹל הָיָה שָׁם	Nun, Gimel, Shin, Hay	"A great miracle happened there"

98

FOCUS ON THE STORY: HANNAH AND HER SEVEN SONS

Chanukah is a story of heroes and bravery. It took great courage to disobey the king and not worship the idols. It took great courage to fight in a war against a powerful enemy the way the Maccabees did.

One of the greatest stories of courage was told in the Book of Maccabees. It is the story of Hannah *(Channah)* and her seven sons. This is the story:

Hannah was the mother of seven sons. She loved each of them very much. They were strong and brave and loyal to God. They would not do as King Antiochus ordered. They would not worship idols.

One day Syrian soldiers came and took away Hannah and her sons. They brought them to the altar of the idol Zeus and ordered them to bow down to the idol and say that the idol was God. But the boys and their mother refused. Then the soldiers killed the oldest son, hoping that when the others saw this, they would worship the idol. But they did not. One after another, the sons were killed, but those who remained would not worship the idol. Finally, Hannah herself was killed. She died declaring her faith in God.

Statue of Zeus (Jupiter) found at Caesarea. Throughout Israel Syrian overlords pressed the Jews to worship before such idols at public altars.

LEARNING MORE ABOUT:
CHANUKAH IN ISRAEL

Chanukah is celebrated as a national holiday in Israel. There is a chanukia on top of almost every public building and synagogue in the country. People take trips to Modin, the city where Mattathias, and Judah and his brothers lived. There they honor the memory of the Maccabees and the great victory that they won.

A special ceremony is held that begins in Modin. First the Israeli flag is raised above the field. Then a large bonfire is lit. A number of torches are lit from the bonfire. These torches are carried

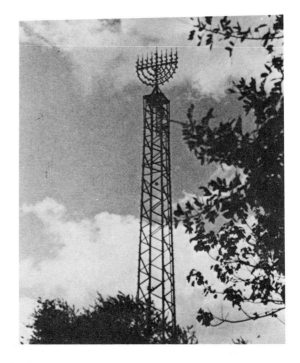

A giant electric menorah lights the skies of Israel for miles around.

The start of the torch-bearing relay race in Israel. The torch of freedom passes from hand to hand.

by runners for a distance. When they come to certain agreed-upon places, they meet other runners who are there waiting for them. The runners who are waiting have unlit torches in their hands. The runners who have come from Modin with their blazing torches light the unlit torches of the second group of runners. The second group of runners run with their torches until they meet up with a third group of runners, who continue to a fourth group, and so on. The last group of runners bring their torches to all the cities of the country. The first torch is brought to Jerusalem, where it is given to the President of Israel. He uses the torch to light Chanukah candles. Then the torch is brought to Mount Zion, where a special memorial service is held for those who died in the Holocaust. The torches are also used to light Chanukah candles at the Western Wall and in all the towns and cities of the country. In this way all the cities and towns in the country are united with Modin, where the story of Chanukah first began.

A group of runners in the torch-bearing relay race.

TU BISHVAT

One day Hadrian, the ruler of Rome, was traveling through his empire. He saw a very, very old man digging in his garden. "What are you doing, old man?" asked the emperor. "I am planting a fig tree," said the old man. "But it takes a long time for a fig tree to grow and bear fruit," said the emperor. "You are a foolish old man. You will be dead by the time the tree bears fruit."

The old man looked at the emperor and replied, "I am planting this tree so that others may enjoy its fruit. Even if I do not live to see it bear fruit, surely my children and grandchildren will benefit from it. Besides, no one knows the future. Perhaps, I myself will live to see this tree bear fruit."

The emperor listened and said, "You are very wise. If you do live to see this tree grow, please let me know. I will reward you for your unselfishness."

Many years later a very, very old man came to the emperor's palace. In his hand was a basket of figs. "I am the old man you saw many years ago planting the fig tree," he said. "I did live to see the fruit of the tree I worked so hard to plant."

The emperor was very happy. He took the basket of figs from the old man's hand and replaced it with a basket of gold.

—Bamidbar Rabbah (Midrash)

In the Hebrew month of *Shevat*, which comes during the cold days of winter, Jews celebrate the New Year of the Trees *(Rosh Hashana La-ilanot)*. How strange it seems to talk of trees and planting when the snow is on the ground, the birds have flown to a warmer place, and you cannot leave your home without a warm coat, boots, gloves, and a hat. But things are different in Israel *(Yisrael)*. In Israel Shevat is the beginning of spring. The ground is soaked from the rains that come in the months before spring. The sun shines brightly. The air is warm. It is just the right time to plant trees. There, on the fifteenth day of Shevat *(Tu* is fifteen in Hebrew), Jews celebrate the New Year of the Trees by planting seedlings which will grow into strong, tall trees.

One of the most important missions of the Jewish National Fund is forest conservation, for trees give shade, fruit, and lumber, and help hold sandy soil in place, thus preventing land erosion.

For many hundreds of years Tu Bishvat has been celebrated by Jews all over the world. Even when our people lived in countries far from Israel, they did not forget that in their homeland the New Year of the Trees was celebrated on this day. Although they could not plant trees in the middle of winter, there were other ways that they could celebrate the holiday. One very important way was to eat the fruit of trees that grew in Israel. So it became the custom to eat such fruits as almonds, raisins, figs, dates, and carob (*charuv* or *bokser*) on Tu Bishvat. It was considered a mitzvah to eat these fruits which grow in Israel and to recite the blessings:

I praise God, who is Lord and Ruler over all,
for creating the fruit of the tree.

בָּרוּךְ אַתָּה יְיָ, אֱלֹהֵינוּ מֶלֶךְ הָעוֹלָם, בּוֹרֵא
פְּרִי הָעֵץ.

I praise God, who is Lord and Ruler over all,
for keeping us well to reach this season.

בָּרוּךְ אַתָּה יְיָ, אֱלֹהֵינוּ מֶלֶךְ הָעוֹלָם, שֶׁהֶחֱיָנוּ
וְקִיְּמָנוּ וְהִגִּיעָנוּ לַזְּמַן הַזֶּה.

Those Jews who live in countries outside of Israel, as well as those who live in Israel, continue to celebrate Tu Bishvat in this way. But another way to celebrate the holiday has been added in recent times. Now that Israel is again a Jewish country, all Jews, all over the world, try to participate in celebrating by planting trees in Israel. Those who live in faraway countries do so by contributing money to plant trees in the forests of

Carefully the youngsters cover the fragile shoots of the saplings. In years to come the wastelands of Israel will burst into foliage with millions of green budding trees.

During the month of Shevat the almond trees embroider the landscape in a sea of snowy white blossoms.

Israel. For a small contribution, the Jewish National Fund will plant a tree in the name of the contributor. Sometimes those who contribute money for the planting of trees have the trees planted in the name of someone else whom they wish to honor. In this way, trees, which are so important to the ecology of Israel, are planted by Jews all over the world.

AN ANCIENT CUSTOM

There was a very beautiful custom followed by the Jews of ancient times. When a baby was born, the parents planted a tree in its honor. The tree was planted on Tu Bishvat following the birth. If the baby was a boy, a cedar tree was planted. If the baby was a girl, a cypress tree was planted. As the children grew big and strong, the trees planted in their honor also grew big and strong. Then, when the children got married, the trees were cut down. The wood from the trees was used to build the chupah, the marriage canopy for the wedding. Just as the wood from the two trees was joined together to form the chupah, so were the bride and groom joined together to form a happy married couple.

TU BISHVAT IN YOUR HOME

Although you do not live in Israel, there are many ways that you and your family can celebrate Tu Bishvat. You can eat the fruit of Israeli trees. You can plant a tree in Israel by contributing to the Jewish National Fund. And you can also plant an indoor garden using very simple materials that you have around the house or can buy

This is the stately cedar. Its wood was used by King Solomon in building the Temple.

easily. Here are some of the things you can do:

1. Fill a jar with water. Put a sweet potato in the jar so that about half of it sticks out above the water. If the mouth of the jar is too large, stick toothpicks around the middle of the sweet potato so that half of it rests in the water and half is above water. Add more water to the jar as it evaporates. Watch it grow. Soon you will have a beautiful green vine.
2. Put a sponge in a small plate. Add enough water to soak the sponge. Scatter bird seed on the sponge. Watch it grow. Add more water as the sponge dries.
3. Cut the top off a carrot. Plant in water or soil in a small plate.
4. Buy a small houseplant. Keep it as your plant. Find out what care it needs. Water it regularly. Watch it grow.

First fruits blossom on a fig tree. The Talmud says: "When one sees a fig tree one should make a blessing, thanking God for creating it."

SOMETHING TO THINK ABOUT

For many hundreds of years after the destruction of the Second Temple, very few Jews lived in Israel. But about one hundred years ago, the Zionist movement was born. Jews began to come back to Israel. They found the country in very poor condition. Much of the land was swamps. The swamps brought insects and the insects brought disease. The new settlers planted trees. The trees helped to dry out the swamps. This is a very important purpose that trees serve. Can you think of any other important uses for trees?

SHARING

Have a Tu Bishvat party. Eat fruit that usually grows in Israel. Recite the blessings.

ON YOUR OWN

Do some research about Israel. Make a list of all the trees that grow there. Report about it to your class.

HEBREW WORDS AND PHRASES:

Below is a list of Hebrew words and phrases relating to Tu Bishvat. See how many you can learn.

טוּ בִּשְׁבָט **Tu Bishvat**	Fifteenth of month of Shevat
רֹאשׁ הַשָּׁנָה לָאִילָנוֹת **Rosh Hashana La-ilanot**	New Year of the Trees
חָרוּב **Charuv**	Carob tree (bokser in Yiddish)
שְׁבָט **Shevat**	Eleventh month of Hebrew calendar

The very first garden in the world was the Garden of Eden. The Bible tells about it in the Book of Genesis. This is what it says: "The Lord God planted a garden in Eden. God planted the garden in the East and placed in it the human being God had made. And from the ground, the Lord God caused to grow every tree that was pleasant to look at and good to eat."

The Garden of Eden as imagined by an artist.

PURIM

There was a Jew in Shushan named Mordecai who brought up his uncle's daughter, Esther. Esther became the queen of King Ahasuerus and he loved her and she found favor in his sight.

In Shushan there lived also a prince named Haman. King Ahasuerus promoted Haman above all the other princes. Haman was angry at Mordecai and because of him wished to harm all the Jews. And Haman said to the king, "There is a people scattered in your land and dispersed in all your provinces whose laws are different from your laws and they do not keep your laws. Let it be written that they be destroyed." And the king said to Haman, "You may do as you wish with these people."

When Mordecai heard about these things he asked Esther to go to the king and plead for her people. Esther was afraid, but she said, "I will go, and if I perish, I perish."

Esther went to the king to plead for her life and the life of her people. "Who is it that will hurt you?" asked the king, "And where can he be found?" And Esther said, "It is wicked Haman."

"And he has built a gallows on which to hang Mordecai," said one of the king's advisors. "Then let Haman be hanged on the gallows and let the Jews be saved," said the king. And Haman was hanged and the Jews were saved.

For that reason Jews rejoice and feast on the fourteenth day of Adar, and they send gifts to the poor.

—Megillat Esther

Purim is the merriest holiday of the Jewish year. It is celebrated on the fourteenth of Adar with carnivals, parties, plays, masquerades, gift-giving, eating, drinking, and silliness. It is the one day of the year when silliness and even drunkenness is encouraged. We are told that we are to get so drunk on this day that we do not know the difference between the words "blessed be Mordecai" and "cursed be Haman."

MEGILLAT ESTHER

The exciting and romantic story of Purim is told in the Bible, in *Megillat Esther*, the Scroll of Esther. It is about a young Jewish woman, *Esther*, who married the king of Persia. As queen, encouraged by the wise and devoted Mordecai, who raised her, she bravely endangered her own life to save her people from the villain *Haman*. You can read an abbreviated version of the story at the beginning of this chapter, or a more

Purim is celebrated with carnivals, parties, and masquerades.

A beautifully illuminated Esther scroll, parchment, seventeenth-century France.

complete version in an English translation of the Megillah. It is a story about courage and faith and hope. And it helped the Jews in times of trouble to believe that a better time would come for them just as it came for the Jews of Persia. In the end, they would be victorious over all their enemies, just as the Jews of Esther's time were victorious over Haman.

Persian soldiers.

READING THE MEGILLAH

The *Megillah* is read in the temple on the evening of Purim. Although it is a religious service, it is a time for having fun and being rowdy. The behavior that is permitted in the temple on Purim at the reading of the Megillah is not allowed at any other time. Many people come to the temple in funny costumes and masks. All the children (and many adults) bring graggers, special Purim noisemakers. As the reader chants the Megillah in the traditional sing-song trope, all listen carefully for

A wall painting from the Dura Europos synagogue. Haman leads Mordecai's horse, and King Ahasuerus and Queen Esther are sitting on their thrones. Dura Europos is a city on the Euphrates River in the northern part of ancient Babylonia.

HAMAN LEADING MORDECAI BEFORE THE THRONE OF AHASUERUS AND ESTHER

111

An ingenious wooden gragger, made in Poland in 1935, depicts Haman and his twentieth-century counterpart, Hitler.

the mention of the name of Haman. When they hear it, they make as much noise as they can with their graggers (*ra-ashanim*). They are trying to blot out the name of Haman. And just as Haman's name is blotted out, Jews hope that all their enemies will be eliminated.

After the service there is usually a party. All sorts of good things are served. But no Purim party would be complete without hamantaschen. These are small three-cornered pastries filled with poppyseeds, prunes, or other fillings. The history of the hamantasch is very interesting. The Jews of Germany used to eat a cake

Purim parties in school must have a king and a beautiful queen, costumes, and tempting refreshments. It's all in the age-old tradition of jolly Purim when anything goes!

filled with poppyseeds on Purim. It was called a mantasch, which means "poppyseed pocket." Since it was served on Purim, it soon came to be called a hamantasch for Haman. The three-cornered shape, it was said, was because Haman wore a three-cornered hat. In Israel, these cakes are called *oznay Haman,* which means "Haman's ears." But whatever you call them, or whatever filling is used, they are delicious.

SHALACH MANOT

One of the most delightful customs of Purim is that of *Shalach Manot,* or exchanging gifts. In the shtetl, the small Jewish town of Eastern Europe, Shalach Manot was a very important ritual. For days before the holiday arrived each home would be filled with the delicious aromas of all sorts of good things being baked. Then, on the morning of Purim, plates of goodies would be prepared. Each plate would be covered with a white napkin. Then the children, usually dressed in costume, would deliver the plates to the homes of neighbors and friends. In each home they would receive a few small coins. What fun the children had. For them it was the best day of the year.

The custom of exchanging Shalach Manot is becoming more and more popular in our country. If your family does not participate in this happy custom, perhaps you would like to introduce it at your home.

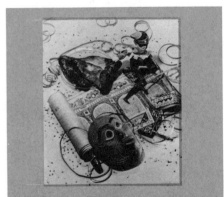

Purim is a time for merrymaking, with masks, graggers, hamantaschen, and Megillah reading.

A Purim Shalach Manot plate. France, eighteenth century.

THE CARNIVAL

Two Israeli stamps with scenes from the Purim Megillah.

In religious schools across the country, Purim is a very busy time. It is the time of the yearly carnival. All the classes have been busy for weeks preparing games of chance and skill. On the Sunday before or after Purim all these games are set up and all the children of the school are invited to play. There are games such as "Pin the Hat on Haman's Head," "Hit Haman in the Nose," "Find Your Way to Shushan," and many, many others. Usually children come in costume and prizes are given for the best costume, the funniest costume, the most original costume, and so on.

Many children (and their parents) consider Purim the best Jewish holiday of the year. "It is too bad," they say, "that it does not come at least every other week."

Purim carnival.

Have a Purim party. Have everyone dress up in costumes and masks. Reenact the story of Purim. Do not use a script. Make up the lines as you go along. Try to make your expression and what you say as funny as possible.

HEBREW WORDS AND PHRASES

Below is a list of Hebrew words and phrases relating to Purim. See how many you can learn.

פּוּרִים	**Purim**	"Lots" (Haman chose the day for attacking the Jews by casting lots)
אֲדָר	**Adar**	Twelfth month of Hebrew calendar
מְגִילָה	**Megillah**	A scroll (book of the Bible)
רַעֲשָׁנִים	**Ra-ashanim**	Noisemakers (graggers in Yiddish)
מִשְׁלוֹחַ מָנוֹת	**Shalach Manot**	Sending portions, gifts, candy
עַדְלֹאיָדַע	**Adloyada**	"until he would not know" (Hebrew name for Purim carnival)
הָמֶנְטַאש	**Hamantasch (Yiddish)**	Purim cake
אֶסְתֵּר	**Esther**	Jewish queen who saved the Jews of Persia
הָמָן	**Haman**	Evil noble who wanted to kill all the Jews
אֲחַשְׁוֵרוֹשׁ	**Ahasuerus**	King of Persia
מָרְדְכַי	**Mordecai**	Cousin of Esther

Everyone in Israel celebrates Purim. It is one of the happiest times of the year. Schoolchildren start preparing weeks in advance. Almost every child wears a costume. Usually these costumes are sewn at home with great care and love. Most families prepare and send Shalach Manot plates covered with Purim delicacies that have been prepared during the week before Purim.

The highlight of the day is the *Adloyada* festival in Tel Aviv. This is a combination festival, parade, and carnival. People come from all over the country to be part of it. The festival gets its

An Adloyada float.

name from the saying in the Talmud that one must get so silly as not to know the difference between the words for "blessed be Mordecai" and "cursed be Haman." The Hebrew words for "not to know the difference" are *Ad lo yada.*

Everyone in Israel is very happy on Purim. Stores and schools are closed, and everyone gets into the spirit of the holiday. Purim has a special meaning to the Jews of Israel. They, too, have enemies who are trying to destroy them. The Purim story gives them hope and faith that in time they too will be victorious over their enemies and that peace will finally come to Israel for all time.

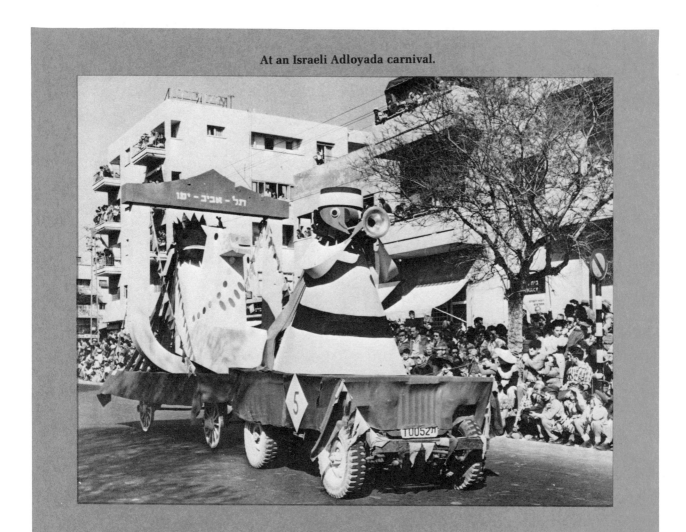

At an Israeli Adloyada carnival.

PASSOVER

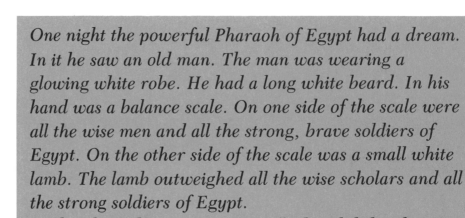

One night the powerful Pharaoh of Egypt had a dream. In it he saw an old man. The man was wearing a glowing white robe. He had a long white beard. In his hand was a balance scale. On one side of the scale were all the wise men and all the strong, brave soldiers of Egypt. On the other side of the scale was a small white lamb. The lamb outweighed all the wise scholars and all the strong soldiers of Egypt.

The Pharaoh was very upset. "What did this dream mean?" he wondered. He called his dream interpreters together. "Tell me what this dream means," he said. But no one could tell him. Finally he called the wisest man in his kingdom, who said, "Your Majesty, we are all in danger. A child will be born to the Children of Israel, who are your slaves. This child will destroy you and all your followers."

"What shall I do to prevent this danger?" asked the Pharaoh. "You must kill all the Jewish babies," answered the wise man. "Then there will not be one who will grow up to lead his people out of Egypt and destroy you."

Pharaoh did as the wise man advised. He ordered all the baby boys of Jewisl mothers to be drowned. Pharaon was happy. "Now I will be safe," he thought.

—Talmudic Aggadah (legend)

The long cold winter is over. Spring has come. The leaves on the trees are beginning to turn green. The spring flowers are beginning to push through the earth. The air is warm and pleasant. The whole world seems happy and glad to be alive.

At home there is excitement and a bustle of activity. The house is being cleaned from top to bottom. Dishes used year-round are being put away, and dishes used for just one week during the year are being taken out and washed. Special foods are being bought and prepared. Everyone is getting ready for *Pesach,* which is celebrated for eight days beginning on the 15th of Nisan. Passover—the holiday of spring, the festival of freedom, the holiday of matzas—is one of the busiest times of the year. All *chametz* (anything made with flour) must be put away. Special foods must be cooked. And all the preparations for the Seder must be made.

THE SEDER

The *Seder* is the highlight of the Passover season. It is more than just a meal. It is a complete service that takes place at home with family and guests seated around the table. The table is set in a special way and special rituals are followed.

This silver Passover plate (Austria, 1807), has three compartments for the three matzot. Decorations: Figures of Moses, Aaron, and Miriam, and three groups of men, carrying small dishes for symbolic Seder foods.

119

Baking and selling matzot during the early 1900's.

In the center of the table is the *Karah*, or Seder plate. On it are bitter herbs, a shankbone, a mixture of apples, nuts, and wine called *charoset*, a roasted egg, and a green vegetable, such as parsley or celery. Each one of these foods stands for something important. The bitter herbs *(maror)* stand for the bitterness of slavery. The shankbone reminds us of the Pesach, or Paschal lamb, that the Israelites ate at their last meal in Egypt. The charoset tastes delicious and looks like the mortar which the Children of Israel used in Egypt to make bricks. The roasted egg stands for the special holiday sacrifice that Jews made on all holidays at the Temple in Jerusalem. The *karpas*, or parsley, represents spring and the new life that this season brings to the earth. It is dipped in salt water to remind the Jews of the tears they shed as slaves in Egypt.

A Passover table set for the Seder. In the center is the Karah. At the head of the table is the cup of Elijah and a Haggadah.

Also in the center of the table is a tray on which there are three whole *matzot* covered with a cloth. Many families now add a fourth matza which they call the Matza of Hope. This fourth matza helps us to remember that there are still Jews who live in countries, such as the Soviet Union and Syria, where they are not free and cannot celebrate Passover as they would like to.

At each person's place there is a wine glass. Four times during the Seder the glass will be filled with wine, the blessing for wine will be recited, and the wine will be drunk. In front of each person is a *Haggadah*. The Haggadah is the book which contains the Seder service. The word Haggadah means "telling," and the Haggadah tells us exactly what we are supposed to do. It also tells us the story of Passover.

THE ORDER OF THE SEDER

The Hebrew word Seder means "order." It refers to the order in which things take place at the Seder. It is very easy to learn how to make a Seder. Even those who have never done it before can follow the instructions in the Haggadah. The same order is used all over the world. So if you follow the order in the Haggadah, you will know that your Seder is just like the one of any Jew anywhere in the world. It is also like the Seder your great-grandparents and great-great-grandparents had.

Israeli stamp with Passover painting showing the baking of matzot.

A medieval drawing showing the baking of matzot. Compare this method to the modern 20th century bakery.

Matzot are watched as they roll along conveyor belts. They must move swiftly and never touch hametz.

121

A Passover plate with the order of the Seder around the rim.

This young man is asking the Four Questions.

This is the order of the Seder:

1. Kaddesh. Recite the Kiddush over the wine.
2. R'Chatz. Wash hands.
3. Karpas. Eat the parsley dipped in salt water—say the blessing.
4. Yachatz. Break the middle matza. Hide one part. It must be eaten at the end of the Seder, so whoever finds it gets a prize.
5. Maggid. Read the story of Passover from the Haggadah.
6. Rachtzah. Wash hands.
7. Motzi Matza. Recite the blessings over the matza and eat the matza.
8. Maror. Bitter herbs.
9. Korech Maror. Combine matza, maror, and charoset and eat together.
10. Shulchan Oruch. Eat dinner.
11. Zaffun. End the meal by eating the afikomen.
12. Barech. Say Grace After Meals.
13. Hallel. Recite Hallel.
14. Nirza. End the service.

THE FOUR QUESTIONS

One of the highlights of the service for the children is the asking of the Four Questions (*Arba Kushyot*). They have been busily learning to ask these questions in Hebrew school for several weeks before Passover, and now they know them perfectly. There are different customs in different families. Sometimes, just the youngest child asks the questions. Other times all the children ask the questions, each one reciting them individually. And in some homes all the children join together to ask the questions in unison.

The Four Questions ask about the customs of the Seder. They ask why we eat matza, why we eat bitter herbs, why we dip the karpas in salt water and the maror in charoset, and why we sit in a reclining position at the Seder. Although the questions are never answered directly, the entire Haggadah, which tells the story of Passover, is really an answer to these questions.

THE STORY OF PASSOVER

The story of Passover is told in the Bible and in the Passover Haggadah. This is how it goes:

Long, long ago the Jews were slaves in Egypt (*Mitzrayim*). They worked very hard to build beautiful palaces and cities for the cruel Pharaoh who ruled over the land. All day long they made bricks and built buildings.

But the *Pharaoh* became more and more cruel. He was afraid that the Hebrew slaves would rise up and rebel against him. So he ordered all the newborn baby boys to be drowned. Without men the Jews would become weaker and weaker, he thought.

One day a beautiful baby boy was born to a Hebrew slave named Yochebed. She did not want him to die. So she thought of a plan. She asked her daughter Miriam to put the baby in a basket and seal the cracks with tar

An ancient Egyptian wall-painting showing prisoners at work making bricks and building a wall.

Stele of King Merneptah of Egypt in which the name of Israel is first mentioned.

A stele is an upright stone slab engraved with an inscription.

A painting discovered on the wall of an Egyptian tomb. The scene shows slaves taking care of cattle. Notice the slave being beaten by an overseer.

An Egyptian brick with the imprint of Pharaoh Rameses II. Rameses II was probably the Pharaoh of the Exodus.

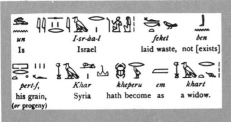

un	I-sr-âa-l		feket	ben
Is	Israel		laid waste,	not [exists]

pert-f,	Khar	kheperu	em	khart
his grain, (or progeny)	Syria	hath become	as	a widow.

Earliest mention of Israel.

The Egyptian text of two lines of Merneptah's stele, a transliteration, and a translation. After the word "Israel," note the figures of a man, a woman, and three straight lines.

so that it would be water-tight. Then she told Miriam to bring the basket down to the Nile River and put it in the bulrushes that grew beside the river. "Perhaps someone will find my baby and save him," she thought. Miriam did as her mother asked. Then she hid herself where she could see the basket and waited to see what would happen.

As Miriam watched, the princess, daughter of the Pharaoh, came to the river to bathe. She saw the baby in the basket and picked it up. "What a beautiful baby," she said. "I will take him back to the palace and raise him as my own child." Miriam ran to the princess. "If you need a good nurse for that baby, I can get someone to take care of him," she said. The princess was delighted. So Miriam ran and got her own mother to be the baby's nurse. And Yochebed was reunited with her baby son.

The princess called the baby Moses (*Moshe*). She raised him in the palace as her own child. He grew up like a prince. But he knew that he was a Jew and that his people were slaves. His mother had taught him that.

One day Moses was in the field. He saw an old Jewish slave working very hard. The old man was very tired. But the Egyptian taskmaster made him work harder and harder. Moses was very angry. Without thinking, he struck the taskmaster with all his might. The Egyptian taskmaster fell down, dead.

Moses could no longer stay in Egypt. He left as fast as he could and wandered for many days in the wilderness. After a while he settled down, got married, and became a shepherd. But he did not forget his people who were slaves in Egypt. He wished that somehow he could save them from their terrible state.

One day Moses was near Mount Horeb watching his sheep. Suddenly he saw a bush. The bush was in flames, but it did not burn up. The longer it burned, the brighter the flames became. Suddenly there was a voice from the burning bush. "Moses," it said. "Take off your shoes. You are on holy ground." Moses took off his shoes and bowed his head. He knew it was the voice of God.

God commanded Moses to return to Egypt. There he was to talk to Pharaoh in God's name and tell him to free the Children of Israel. Moses took his brother Aaron (*Aharon*) and went to the palace of the Pharaoh. There they told the Pharaoh what God had said. But Pharaoh was not afraid of the God of Moses. He would not let the Hebrews go free.

Moses and Aaron left the palace. But the next day terrible things began to happen to the Egyptians. First all the water turned to blood. Then grasshoppers and insects swarmed all over the country. Then there were frogs all over and darkness and hail. All together there were ten plagues, or terrible things, that happened to the Egyptians. The last was the worst of all. All the first-born children of the Egyptians died. But no Jews died. The plague passed over the Jewish homes. Pharaoh agreed to let the Jews leave Egypt.

That night the Hebrews left Egypt. But before they left they celebrated an important ritual, the Passover feast. Each family roasted a lamb. Then they had a family feast at which the lamb was eaten with matza and bitter herbs.

After the Passover feast the Israelites left Egypt. They traveled until they came to the Sea of Reeds, or the Red Sea. But Pharaoh had changed his mind. He

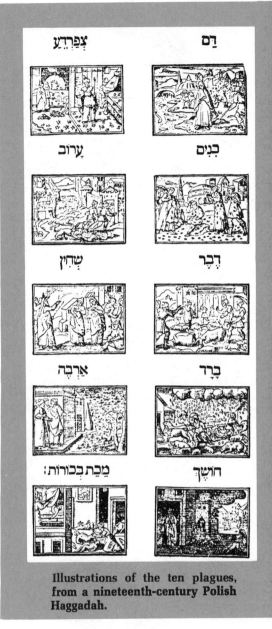

Illustrations of the ten plagues, from a nineteenth-century Polish Haggadah.

The Pharaohs of Egypt left many monuments. They built temples, monuments, pyramids, and statues of themselves and their gods. This is a gigantic statue of a Pharaoh. It is about 40 feet tall and weighs many tons.

Present-day Samaritans in Israel, who claim descent from the tribes of Ephraim and Manasseh, have their own customs. Here they bake matzot for Passover.

wanted the Israelites to come back. He wanted them to continue to be his slaves and work for him. So he led his soldiers after them. At the Sea of Reeds he caught up with them. The people were frightened. They were afraid they would die in the wilderness or be forced to return to Egypt. But God was with them. As they stepped into the Sea of Reeds, the water separated into two walls and they walked across on dry land. When the Egyptians tried to follow, the waters closed again as they had been before.

The Children of Israel were safe on shore. Pharaoh and his mighty army drowned in the sea. The people rejoiced. They sang and danced and offered prayers to God. Then they started their long journey to the promised land.

FAMILY SHARING

The Seder is a happy celebration. Everyone reads the Haggadah together. Happy songs are sung and a delicious meal is eaten. Before the meal is served, the ritual foods are eaten and the blessings are recited:

ON EATING MATZA

I praise God, who is Lord and Ruler over all,
for bringing forth bread from the earth.

בָּרוּךְ אַתָּה יְיָ, אֱלֹהֵינוּ מֶלֶךְ הָעוֹלָם, הַמּוֹצִיא
לֶחֶם מִן הָאָרֶץ.

I praise God, who is Lord and Ruler over all,
for teaching us the commandment of eating matza.

בָּרוּךְ אַתָּה יְיָ, אֱלֹהֵינוּ מֶלֶךְ הָעוֹלָם, אֲשֶׁר
קִדְּשָׁנוּ בְּמִצְוֹתָיו, וְצִוָּנוּ עַל־אֲכִילַת מַצָּה.

126

ON BITTER HERBS

I praise God, who is Lord and Ruler over all,
for teaching us the commandment of eating bitter
* herbs.*

בָּרוּךְ אַתָּה יְיָ, אֱלֹהֵינוּ מֶלֶךְ הָעוֹלָם, אֲשֶׁר
קִדְּשָׁנוּ בְּמִצְוֹתָיו, וְצִוָּנוּ עַל־אֲכִילַת מָרוֹר.

THE CUP OF ELIJAH

At the Seder, each person drinks four cups of wine. But a fifth cup of wine is also poured. That *Kos Eliyahu* is for Elijah the Prophet. Elijah lived many, many years ago. The Bible tells us that he did many wonderful and miraculous deeds. There have been many legends about him and all the wonderful things he could do. According to one of the legends, Elijah will come back to earth. When he comes, it will be the beginning of a golden age. The whole world will be at peace, and all people will love each other and be good to each other.

When we fill the fifth cup of wine at the Seder for Elijah, we are saying that we hope the wonderful time Elijah will announce will come soon, and that all people will soon learn to live together in peace.

THE AFIKOMEN

After the meal is finished, everyone eats a piece of the *afikomen*. This is the dessert that marks the end of the meal. It is a piece of the middle of the three matzot placed on the table with the other ritual foods. According to custom, the meal must end with the eating of the afikomen, and no food is eaten at the Seder afterwards. So you can see that this particular piece of matza is very important and very special.

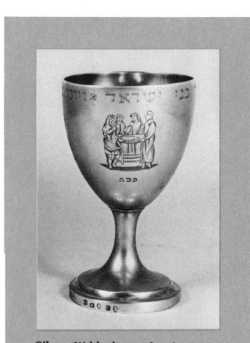

Silver Kiddush cup for festivals. Passover Eve scene shows figures standing around table with Paschal Lamb as prescribed in Exodus 12:11.

Ancient Haggadah manuscript found in Cairo, Egypt.

127

A delightful custom has developed in connection with the afikomen. Early in the Seder, the Seder leader hides the afikomen for safekeeping so that he or she will know exactly where to find it at the end of the meal. The children at the Seder compete to find the matza and hide it so that the Seder leader cannot find it. At the end of the meal, when the matza is to be eaten, the leader must redeem it from the culprit for a reward.

Of course, this is all done in the spirit of fun, and it helps to make the Seder even more enjoyable for all.

SOMETHING TO THINK ABOUT

Passover has four names. Each one is related to one of the meanings of the holiday. See if you can tell how each one tells something about what the holiday means. The names of the holiday are:

חַג הַפֶּסַח *Chag Hapesach*—The Holiday of the Paschal Lamb

חַג הָאָסִיף *Chag Haasif*—The Holiday of Spring

חַג הַמַצוֹת *Chag Hamatzot*—The Holiday of Matzot

זְמַן חֵרוּתֵינוּ *Zman Cherutenu*—The Season of Our Freedom

SHARING FEELINGS

During one part of the Seder, we recite the ten plagues that the Egyptians suffered. As we mention each plague, we pour a drop of wine from our glass. We are told that this is done because our cup of happiness cannot be completely full when anyone suffers—even an enemy. Do you think this is a right way to feel? Can you feel this way about people who are mean to you? Share your feelings with a friend in your class.

ON YOUR OWN

Learn to ask the Four Questions. If you cannot learn all of it in Hebrew, learn as much as you can in Hebrew and the rest in English.

Below is a list of Hebrew words and phrases relating to Passover. See how many you can learn.

Hebrew	Transliteration	Meaning
כַּרְפַּס	**Karpas**	Parsley
פֶּסַח	**Pesach**	Passover
נִיסָן	**Nisan**	First month of Hebrew calendar
חָמֵץ	**Chametz**	Leavened food (made with flour)
מַצָּה	**Matza**	Unleavened bread
מָרוֹר	**Maror**	Bitter herbs
חֲרוֹסֶת	**Charoset**	Mixture of chopped apples, nuts, wine, and cinnamon
אֲפִיקוֹמָן	**Afikomen**	Greek word meaning "dessert"
סֵדֶר	**Seder**	The Passover service
כּוֹס אֵלִיָהוּ	**Kos Eliyahu**	Cup of Elijah
אַרְבַּע קוּשְׁיוֹת	**Arba Kushyot**	Four Questions (word really means "difficulties") (feer kashes in Yiddish)
הַגָּדָה	**Haggadah**	"The telling" (of the Pesach story)
קְעָרָה	**Karah**	Compartmented Seder plate
פַּרְעֹה	**Pharaoh**	King of Egypt who enslaved the Hebrews
מֹשֶׁה	**Moshe**	Moses, the leader and prophet of Israel
אַהֲרֹן	**Aharon**	Aaron, the brother of Moses
מִצְרַיִם	**Mitzrayim**	Egypt

FOCUS ON: THE VALUES
OF PASSOVER

The holiday of Passover teaches us many important Jewish values. Here are some of them:

1. Slavery is wrong. No group should make slaves of another.

2. The Haggadah says: "Let all who are hungry come and eat." It is the duty of all Jews to see that others do not go hungry.

3. Families should celebrate together.

4. All Jews are loyal to Israel. In the Haggadah we say, "Next year in Jerusalem."

5. The Jewish tradition should be passed down from one generation to the next.

Samaritans at the Seder. Can you recognize the foods they are serving?

Preparations for Passover in the shtetl started immediately after Purim. The wine for Passover had to be made and new clothes had to be ordered from the tailor for each member of the family. Matzot were baked in matza factories. Each family would bring its own flour to the bakery and pay the baker to make matzot especially for them.

For families who were too poor to buy flour and pay the baker to make matzot for them, there was a special fund to take care of these needs. The fund was called

A Jew carrying matzot for delivery in an East European shtetl.

Maot Chitim. Its name means "money for wheat." Before Passover the rabbi of the community and a committee of wealthy persons went from house to house collecting for the fund. Everyone who was able to, contributed.

The schoolchildren loved Passover. For two weeks before the holiday started, they attended school for only half a day. Even the time that they did attend was spent learning about the holiday. The children did not consider this as tedious as their regular lessons,

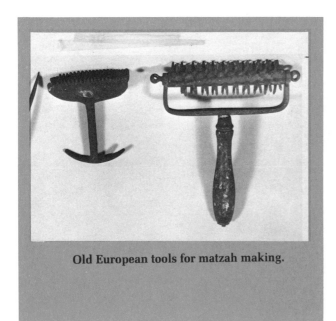

Old European tools for matzah making.

in which they repeated the words of the Bible and Talmud over and over until they knew them by heart.

In the home the housewives were busy scrubbing and cleaning. Not a bit of chametz (leaven) could remain in the house. Different dishes were kept for Passover. These were removed from the places where they were stored and were washed. The dishes used all year were stored away until after the holiday was over. All the food for the Seder was cooked. The aromas coming from each home were delightful and promised a delicious feast to come.

On the night of the first Seder, the table was beautifully set with all the ritual foods. The entire family was seated around the table. The father was seated on a large chair on which had been placed a cushion. This was to show that he was like a king, not a slave.

The next night there was a second Seder celebrated with the same festivity as the first. For eight days this wonderful holiday continued. When it was over the members of the family wished each other a happy and healthy summer to come and began the job of storing away the Passover dishes for another year.

LAG B'OMER

It was a sad time for the people of Israel. Their country was ruled by Rome. The Romans did not allow the Jews to study the Torah. There were many great scholars who were excellent teachers. But they were not permitted to teach. The punishment for teaching or studying Torah was death.

One of the great scholars of that time was Rabbi Simon Bar Yohai. He continued to study and teach the Torah. But he was in great danger. His students were very worried about him. They wanted to continue their studies, but they knew that they and their teacher were in danger. "You must go and hide," they said. "You must go somewhere where the Romans will not be able to find you. Go to the hills. There are caves there, so you will be able to study Torah without being caught by the Romans."

"But what about you, my students?" asked Rabbi Simon. "How will you be able to find me so that you may continue your studies?" "We will find you," said the students.

Rabbi Simon hid in a cave. There he studied Torah all day long. When his students thought it was safe, they went to the hills to find him. But there were Roman soldiers all over. They would have to think of a way to fool the soldiers. So they carried bows and arrows with them. When they were stopped by the soldiers, they said, "We are going to have a picnic and then we will go hunting."

The students found Rabbi Simon in his hiding place. All day they studied Torah with him. Then they went home. Each morning after that, they packed a picnic lunch and bows and arrows. Each time they were stopped, they told the soldiers they were going hunting and on a picnic. And each day they went to Rabbi Simon Bar Yohai's cave to study Torah with him.

—Aggadah

Have you ever been on a *Lag B'Omer* picnic? It is usually sponsored by a Hebrew or religious school. Sometimes several schools get together and hold a joint picnic. There are baseball games, relay races, and, of course, lots of good picnic food. The picnic is usually lots of fun, and usually it is the last social get-together of the religious-school year before summer vacation.

The celebration of Lag B'Omer in this way is becoming more and more popular in our country. But the background and meaning of the day itself is a mystery long lost in ancient history. When was this day first celebrated? Why was it celebrated? We do not really know. But we will explore what we do know about this day, which is celebrated as a sort of "half-holiday."

Lag B'Omer campfire.

THE COUNTING OF THE OMER

Long, long ago, the Jews were farmers. Their lives centered around the planting and harvesting cycle. Many Jewish customs originated at that time. Most of the holidays that we still celebrate began as planting or harvesting festivals.

Passover was the season of the wheat harvest. There was a second harvest of the barley on Shavuot. Both of these harvest periods were very important. If the crops failed, there would be no food to eat. So special religious ceremonies developed in which the Jews prayed for a good harvest. One of the things the farmers did was to bring a sacrifice to the Temple each day during the waiting period from one harvest to the next. The sacrifice or offering was a portion of barley from their fields. The

An ancient stone jug used for storing grain. It can hold an omer.

Three times a year (Sukkot, Pesach, and Shavuot) the Jews of ancient Israel would march on foot to the Holy Temple in Jerusalem. Today in modern Israel, the age-old ceremony is re-enacted. Here pilgrims ascend Mount Zion to the blowing of the shofars.

A nineteenth-century European Omer calendar. The numbers, top to bottom, indicate that this is the thirty-third day of the Omer (Lag B'Omer), or four weeks and five days since the beginning of the seven-week period between Passover and Shavuot.

Hadrian, Roman emperor (117–138), who suppressed Bar Kochba's revolt against Roman tyranny.

barley was measured by the Omer, a special measure at that time. There would then be certain prayers and rituals that they performed. One of the rituals was to count off each day of the waiting period between harvests. They called it counting the days of the *Omer*. Since the Hebrew word for counting is Sefirah, we sometimes call these *Sefirah* Days. The counting of the Omer begins on the second day of Passover. It ends forty-nine days later on the first day of Shavuot.

The Sefirah Days were very sacred days in ancient times. The Jews, like all farmers everywhere, worried a lot about their harvest. Would it be a good harvest? Would the crops be plentiful? Would the grain be eaten by insects? And so on. It was not a time for rejoicing. It was a very serious time. Many things were forbidden. No marriages or other special ceremonies could take place. There could not be any gaiety or fun. There were only two days on which the rules were relaxed. One was Rosh Chodesh. Lag B'Omer was the other.

Lag B'Omer is the thirty-third day of the Omer. The name comes from the Hebrew letters for thirty-three. Lamed stands for thirty, and Gimel stands for three. Lag B'Omer comes each year on the eighteenth day of Iyar. We do not really know why things were different on Lag B'Omer, but there were some events in the later history of the Jews that were said to be the reason. You will read about them in the next section.

THE SCHOLAR'S HOLIDAY

About two thousand years ago Israel was ruled by Rome. The Romans were very cruel to the Jews. They taxed them heavily. And they would not permit them to study Torah on pain of death. But the study of Torah

Yigal Yadin, the Israel archaeologist, discovered letters from Bar Kochba in this cave in the Judean desert.

An Israeli stamp in honor of Bar Kochba.

went on anyway in spite of these restrictions. One of the great teachers of that time was *Rabbi Akiva*. Rabbi Akiva had many brave students who continued to study Torah. They were not afraid of the Romans.

From time to time the Jews rebelled against Roman rule. One of these rebellions was led by a great Jewish hero named *Bar Kochba.* Most of the young men who volunteered to fight in his army were students of Rabbi Akiva. They lost many battles. The armies of Rome were very powerful. But Bar Kochba did win a great victory on Lag B'Omer. The students and scholars who were his soldiers rejoiced. That is one of the reasons given for rejoicing on Lag B'Omer. Another reason given is that a terrible disease broke out among the students of Rabbi Akiva. Many young men died. But on Lag B'Omer the disease suddenly stopped. That is why we celebrate.

Coin of the Bar Kochba period. The ancient Hebrew reads, "First year of the redemption of Israel" and "Simeon, Nasi of Israel."

Israeli stamp with Lag B'Omer scene. This picture was painted by the Israeli artist Reuven Rubin and is entitled "Dancers of Meron."

There is another great scholar who is remembered on Lag B'Omer. His name was *Rabbi Simon Bar Yohai.* He also continued to teach the Torah when the Romans did not allow it. He hid in a cave so that the Romans would not find or disturb him. His students would come to the cave to study with him. To deceive the Romans they would carry bows and arrows and pretend that they were going hunting. Rabbi Simon died on Lag B'Omer. But what is remembered on this day is not his death, but the good life he led. Chasidim who live in Israel visit his grave on this day and sing and dance in honor of this great scholar.

YOM HAMOREH

In our own time Lag B'Omer has become a time to honor teachers. On this day Hebrew and religious schools all over the country celebrate *Yom Hamoreh,* the Day of the Teacher. Special assemblies and parties are held, and often awards are given to favorite teachers or to teachers who have served in the field of Jewish education for a number of years. It is a special day set aside to tell our teachers how important they are to us and how much we love them.

Tiberias, Israel, and the tomb of Rabbi Meir Baal Ha-Nes, member of the Sanhedrin, and pupil of Rabbi Akiba. In the background: the Sea of Galilee.

Lag B'Omer has been given new importance in our time by making it a time to celebrate Yom Hamoreh, the Day of the Teacher. Do you think it is important to set aside a day to honor religious-school and Hebrew-school teachers? Why are teachers important? What can you do to honor your teacher?

ON YOUR OWN

Make a Yom Hamoreh greeting card for your Hebrew school teacher. On it tell your teacher what makes him or her special. Decorate the card and send it to your teacher.

HEBREW WORDS AND PHRASES

Below is a list of Hebrew words and phrases relating to Lag B'Omer. See how many you can learn.

Hebrew		English
לַ״ג בָּעוֹמֶר	**Lag B'Omer**	Thirty-third day of the counting of the Omer
עוֹמֶר	**Omer**	Sheaf, measure
לָמֶד	**Lamed**	Hebrew letter with the value of 30
גִימֶל	**Gimel**	Hebrew letter with the value of 3
סְפִירָה	**Sefirah**	Time of Counting the Omer
בַּר־כּוֹכְבָא	**Bar Kochba**	Leader of the Jewish revolt against Rome (132–135 C.E.)
רַבִּי שִׁמְעוֹן בַּר יוֹחַאי	**Rabbi Simon Bar Yohai**	Scholar, teacher, and student of Rabbi Akiva
יוֹם הַמוֹרֶה	**Yom Hamoreh**	The Day of the Teacher
רַבִּי עֲקִיבָא	**Rabbi Akiva**	Great Jewish teacher

SHAVUOT

When the mountains heard that God was about to present the Torah to the Children of Israel, they began to quarrel among themselves. Each one wanted to be the one from whose top God would give the Torah.

Mount Tabor said, "Surely I deserve the honor of having God give the Torah from my peak. I am the highest mountain. When the whole world was covered by water and Noah's Ark floated above the water, only my peak could be seen."

"Oh, no," said Mount Hermon. "I will be the mountain that is chosen. When the Israelites crossed the Red Sea, I helped to keep the waters separated."

Mount Carmel did not say anything. But it was confident that it would be chosen by God for the honor. After all, wasn't it tall and beautiful, looking out over the sea?

Mount Sinai did not join in the quarrel. It was just a small mountain. Surely it would not be chosen for this great honor. But it was wrong. God gave the Torah from the top of Mount Sinai because it was modest and did not quarrel with the other mountains.

—Aggadah

In the last chapter you read that *Shavuot* is a harvest holiday. It is called *Chag Hakatzir,* the Holiday of the Ingathering. It is the time of the eagerly awaited second barley harvest. You learned that it comes exactly fifty days after Passover (in other words, on the sixth day of Sivan). The word Shavuot means "Weeks" because this is seven weeks after Passover.

But like all Jewish holidays, Shavuot has a historical meaning as well as an agricultural one. Shavuot is the time when Jews celebrate the giving of the Torah on Mount Sinai *(z'man matan Toratenu).* The Bible tells the story of the giving of the Ten Commandments *(Aseret HaDibrot)* in dramatic terms. In the Book of Exodus, chapters 19 and 20, we are told that:

In the third month after the Children of Israel left Egypt they came to the wilderness of Sinai. There they camped in front of the mountain. And Moses went up to God. And the Lord called to him from the mountain, saying, "You shall say to the Children of Israel: 'You saw what I did to the Egyptians and how I saved you and brought you to me. Now if you will listen to my voice and obey my laws, you will be my treasure from among all peoples.' "

And Moses told the people what God had said. And the people answered, "All that the Lord has said, we will do."

A photograph of Mount Sinai. It was on top of this mountain that Moses received the Ten Commandments.

Wood engraving of the Ten Commandments.

This picture from the world-famous Sarajevo Haggadah shows Moses on Mount Sinai with the Ten Commandments. Around the foot of the mountain the Israelites await Moses.

A relief is a deep carving on a flat surface. This stone relief of the holy Ark was found in the ancient synagogue at Capernaum, (Kfar Nahum), Israel. The carving is about 2,500 years old.

All the people sanctified themselves and waited for the Torah. And there was thunder and lightning, and a thick cloud surrounded the mountain. Then the sound of a shofar blowing very loudly was heard and the people trembled. Soon the mountain was completely surrounded by smoke and flames, the shofar got louder and louder, and the whole mountain shook.

Then God spoke the words, saying:

1. *I am the Lord, your God.*
2. *You shall have no other gods before me.*
3. *You shall not take the name of the Lord in vain.*
4. *Remember the Sabbath to keep it holy.*
5. *Honor your father and your mother.*
6. *You shall not kill.*
7. *You shall not be unfaithful to wife or husband.*
8. *You shall not steal.*
9. *You shall not bear false witness.*
10. *You shall not desire what is your neighbor's.*

CELEBRATING SHAVUOT

A number of special customs have developed through the years for celebrating Shavuot. Services are held in the temple. A very beautiful poem called *Akdamut*, which glorifies God, is recited. The Book of *Ruth* from the Bible is read. This book tells about the dedication and love of Ruth, a convert to Judaism. It contains the famous quotation, "Ask me not to leave you. For where you go, I will go. Your people will be my people and your God will be my God." Those words were said by Ruth to her mother-in-law after her husband died. Perhaps you will want to read the rest of this very interesting book of the Bible.

At home Shavuot is celebrated by decorating the home with freshly cut flowers and branches to symbolize the harvest. Special foods are eaten which are made with milk and cheese. Such dishes as blintzes, pirogen, and cheesecake have become traditional for this holiday. As with most foods that are eaten on holidays, we do not really know how the custom of eating them originated.

In many religious schools there is a *Bikkurim* festival for the children. They march in a procession wearing lovely costumes and carrying baskets of fruit which they place on the pulpit of the sanctuary. The fruit is later donated to hospitals or to the poor. This custom is to remind us of the first fruits of the field which the Jews brought to the Temple in ancient times as an offering to God. The first fruits were called Bikkurim.

Israeli stamp in honor of Shavuot.

A bikkurim pageant on a kibbutz in Israel. The Hebrew sign reads: 'Omer Omer, New Grain."

145

CONFIRMATION

Something new has been added to the festival of Shavuot in recent times. It has become the time when boys and girls are confirmed. This is a ceremony that was introduced in Reform temples to honor those students who continued to study in the religious school after their Bar or Bat Mitzvah. It usually takes place at age fifteen or sixteen, when they graduate from religious school and are accepted into the congregation. This ceremony gives added meaning to an ancient holiday.

Young men and women being confirmed in the temple.

Read the Book of Ruth in the Bible. You will find the story very interesting. Write a book report on the book. In it tell the story and also what you think the story means.

SHARING

Learn to prepare a dairy food that is traditional for Shavuot, such as blintzes. Make enough for your classmates and share it with them.

HEBREW WORDS AND PHRASES

Below is a list of Hebrew words and phrases relating to Shavuot. See how many you can learn.

Hebrew	Transliteration	Meaning
שָׁבוּעוֹת	**Shavuot**	Weeks
זְמַן מַתַּן תּוֹרָתֵינוּ	**Z'man matan toratenu**	Time of the giving of our Torah
חַג הַבִּכּוּרִים	**Chag Habikkurim**	Festival of First Fruits
סְפִירָה	**Sefirah**	Counting (of the Omer)
חַג הַקָּצִיר	**Chag Hakatzir**	Harvest Festival
עֲשֶׂרֶת הַדִּבְּרוֹת	**Aseret Hadibrot**	Ten Commandments
אַקְדָמוּת	**Akdamut**	Special Shavuot prayer
מְגִלַּת־רוּת	**Megillat Ruth**	Book of Ruth
בִּכּוּרִים	**Bikkurim**	First Fruits

The season of Shavuot was a very happy one in the shtetl for several reasons. It was the beginning of summer, and the world is particularly beautiful at that time. It was the end of the period of counting the Omer, the Sefirah period, during which no weddings and other festivities were allowed. And it celebrated the giving of the Torah, one of the most important religious experiences in the history of the Jewish people.

The children were especially happy on Shavuot. School was in session for only half a day for the four days before Shavuot, and of course there was no school at all on Shavuot itself.

In every home, families were busy preparing for the holiday. Special dairy foods were prepared. From every house one could smell the delicious aromas of blintzes frying and cheesecake baking. Homes were decorated with flowers, leaves, and branches in honor of the season. The synagogues, too, were decorated with leaves and branches.

On Shavuot evening, the men spent the entire night at the synagogue studying and waiting for the sun to rise. There is an interesting legend connected with this. When God was first made known on Mount Sinai, it was early in the morning. The Jews were still asleep and had to be awakened. Jews since then have stayed awake all night on Shavuot to show that if God were giving the Torah at this time, all the Jews would be awake and ready to receive it.

On Shavuot evening the men of the shtetl spent the entire night in the synagogue studying and waiting for the sun to rise. This is a painting by the Jewish artist, Isidor Kaufmann.

TISHA B'AV

By the rivers of Babylon we sat and cried when we remembered Zion. We left our harps on the willow trees there. For those who led us as captives from our country asked us to sing. Our tormentors asked us to be happy and sing one of the songs of Zion.

How can we sing the Lord's song in a foreign land? If I forget you, O Jerusalem, let my right hand loose its usefulness. Let my tongue stick to the roof of my mouth, if I do not remember you. If I do not set Jerusalem above my greatest joy.

—Psalm 137

A copy of the carving on the Arch of Titus, showing the Menorah and other furniture of the Temple being carried in triumph through the streets of Rome.

Model of a centurion, commander of a hundred Roman soldiers.

The sad poem at the beginning of this chapter was written about a terrible event in Jewish history. In the year 586 B.C.E. the Babylonians conquered Jerusalem (*Yerushalayim*). Babylonian soldiers marched into the holy city of the Jews. They destroyed the Temple (*Bet Hamikdash*). Then they took many of the strong young men and women captive. They forced them to leave their families and their country and go to Babylonia to live. There they would not be able to organize a rebellion against their captors. These events are known in history as the Babylonian Exile or the Babylonian Captivity. According to tradition they happened on the ninth day of the month of Av.

Many years later, the Jews managed to regain their land. The Temple had been rebuilt. But once again tragedy came. In 70 C.E., about six hundred years after the Babylonian Exile, Rome conquered Jerusalem. Once again, the Temple was destroyed. Once again, Jerusalem was destroyed. And according to tradition, this tragedy, too, came on the ninth day (*Tisha*) of *Av*. Is it any wonder that the ninth day of the Hebrew month of Av (*Tisha B'Av* in Hebrew) became a day of sadness and mourning for Jews all over the world?

A battering ram. Rams such as this were brought up to the walls of Jerusalem and used to punch holes in the stone wall. Once a hole was opened, enemy soldiers poured in and captured the city.

TISHA B'AV CUSTOMS

The ninth day of Av is a universal day of Jewish mourning. On it Jews remember not only the destruction of the First and Second Temples. They also mourn other national disasters, such as the defeat of *Bar Kochba* at Betar and the Spanish Inquisition. Many Jews fast on this day and attend services. In the temple the service is usually held in semi-darkness. Only the light from the eternal light (*Ner Tamid*) or from memorial candles is visible. The Book of Lamentations is read as part of the service. This book, traditionally written by the prophet *Jeremiah*, is very sad. It tells about the destruction of Jerusalem and the First Temple. Not only are the words sad, but the trope or chant in which it is read has a sad and mournful sound. In some temples the worshippers sit on backless benches or on the floor as a sign of mourning.

Some Jews observe the nine days before Tisha B'Av as a mourning period. During that time they do not buy new clothes, take haircuts, go swimming, or eat meat.

To celebrate the capture of Jerusalem the Roman conquerors built an arch in Rome. This monument is called the Arch of Titus.

An artist's conception of the Bet Hamikdash, the Temple in Jerusalem. The large area, the Temple Mount, was surrounded by a wall.

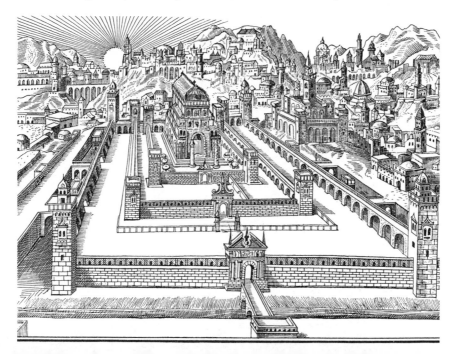

TISHA B'AV IN MODERN ISRAEL

The Western Wall in the Old City of Jerusalem is all that remains of the Second Temple.

In the past few years, since 1967, a new custom has developed among many of the Jews in Israel. In 1967, after the Six Day War, Jerusalem was reunited under Jewish rule after almost two thousand years. Since that time it has become the practice for Israelis to travel from all over the country to Jerusalem. There they gather around the Western Wall *(Kotel Hamaaravi)*, an original wall of the gate surrounding the Temple in ancient times. The years of sadness have given way to great happiness. Jerusalem has been restored as a Jewish city.

SOMETHING TO THINK ABOUT

Many Jews in Israel celebrate Tisha B'Av as a day of joy because Jerusalem is now reunited under Israeli rule. Do you think it is right to give this mourning day a new meaning? Why?

ON YOUR OWN

Listen to the *Jeremiah Symphony* by Leonard Bernstein. Parts of it were inspired by the Book of Lamentations, the sad book of the Bible that is read on Tisha B'Av. See if you can guess which those parts are.

HEBREW WORDS AND PHRASES

Below is a list of Hebrew words and phrases relating to Tisha B'Av. See how many you can learn.

תִּשְׁעָה בְּאָב	**Tisha B'Av**	Ninth day of the month of Av
אָב	**Av**	Eleventh month of the Jewish calendar
תִּשְׁעָה	**Tisha**	Nine
בַּר־כּוֹכְבָא	**Bar Kochba**	Leader of the revolt against Rome
כּוֹתֶל־הַמַעֲרָבִי	**Kotel Hamaravi**	Western Wall, the last remnant of the Holy Temple in Jerusalem
יְרוּשָׁלַיִם	**Yerushalayim**	Jerusalem
נֵר־תָּמִיד	**Ner Tamid**	Eternal Light
בֵּית־הַמִקְדָּשׁ	**Bet Hamikdash**	The Holy Temple

The custom of fasting—that is, not eating any food at all for a period of time—goes back to ancient days. In the days of the Temple, the Jews would fast if they were afraid that some disaster would come. If it seemed that there would be a famine, a plague, or a war, the people fasted and prayed to God. They would dress themselves in sackcloth, put ashes on their heads, and walk in a procession to the Temple. As they walked they would cry out loud. When they reached the Temple, they would throw themselves down in front of the altar and pray to God that the terrible thing they feared would not happen.

Through the years, special fast-days were declared and the Jews fasted just on those days. Usually the fast-day was to commemorate a very sad event that had happened on that particular date at one time in the history of the Jews. In the shtetl, many Jews fasted on all of these special fast-days.

In our time, most Jews fast on Yom Kippur. Some Jews fast on Tisha B'Av to remember all the sad things in Jewish history that that day commemorates. Only a few Jews still fast on all the other fast-days.

Up above the Aron Ha-Kodesh hangs a light which is never permitted to go out. The Ner Tamid, the "eternal light," is the symbol of the presence of God among us. In the days of the Temple, a lamp containing pure olive oil burned continuously before the Ark.

The Ner Tamid is an ever burning reminder of our heritage and our links to the ancient Temple.

The Tisha B'Av service is usually held in semi-darkness. Only the light from the ever burning Ner Tamid is visible.

YOM HASHOAH AND YOM HAATZMAUT

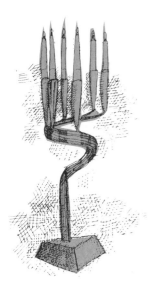

Once there were two brothers who loved each other very much. Both of them were farmers. One was married and had a lovely family. The other was single. They lived several miles apart on opposite ends of their farm. But they saw each other often.

One day, after he had gathered his harvest, the unmarried brother had an idea. "My brother is married and has a large family," he thought. "His needs are greater than mine. I will give a portion of the grain I harvested to him and his family." He loaded a large portion of his harvest on a wagon and set out to his brother's home.

That same day, the married brother had gathered his harvest. He, too, had an idea. "I have so much," he thought to himself. "I have a wife and lovely children. I am very fortunate. But my brother does not have a wife to love him. He does not have children. I will bring him a part of my harvest as a gift. That will make him feel better." So he loaded a large portion of his harvest on a wagon and set out to his brother's home.

Midway between their two homes, the two brothers met. Each told the other what he was doing. The two brothers embraced. They cried and laughed together. Then each went back to his own home.

God watched as all this was happening. "What a beautiful show of love this is," thought God. "On this spot will someday stand the city of Jerusalem."

—Aggadah

Most Jewish holidays are very old. They originated long before the days of recorded history. Until recent times the newest Jewish holiday was Chanukah. But even Chanukah is two thousand years old. Now there are two new days on the Jewish calendar. Your grandparents did not observe these days when they were young. They couldn't. The events that these days commemorate are so new that they were just taking place when your grandparents were children. But they were very important events—events that will change the course of Jewish history for all time. The two events were the Holocaust and the establishment of the State of Israel. We remember the Holocaust on Yom Hashoah, and we celebrate the declaration of the State of Israel on Yom Haatzmaut.

THE HOLOCAUST

The word Holocaust *(shoah)* means destruction. It is used to describe the most terrible event that ever happened—not just in Jewish history, but in all history. It was the time when a German madman named Hitler and his followers, the Nazis, killed six million Jews. These people were killed for no other reason than that they were Jews.

Israeli stamp to preserve the memory of those who died in the War of Liberation.

156

It is almost impossible to imagine the taking of six million lives. You know how precious your life is to you. You know how dear the lives of those you love are. You know how sad you are when you hear or read about one person dying. Six million people died in the Holocaust. There is hardly a Jewish family anywhere that did not lose a relative or a friend in that terrible destruction. As much as we would like to forget the horrible events of the Holocaust, it is important to remember. We must never allow something so awful to happen again.

The Nazis forced all Jews to wear a yellow star with the word jude (Jew) on it. Any Jew caught not wearing this symbol was immediately executed.

YOM HASHOAH

Yom Hashoah, or Holocaust Remembrance Day, is observed on the twenty-seventh day of the month of *Nisan.* On that day we remember all the events of the Holocaust. We remember those who died *al kiddush Hashem,* for the sanctification of God's name. We remember all those who died silently—who were not able to resist. We also remember those who tried to

A Jewish family wearing their yellow stars are led off to the concentration camp.

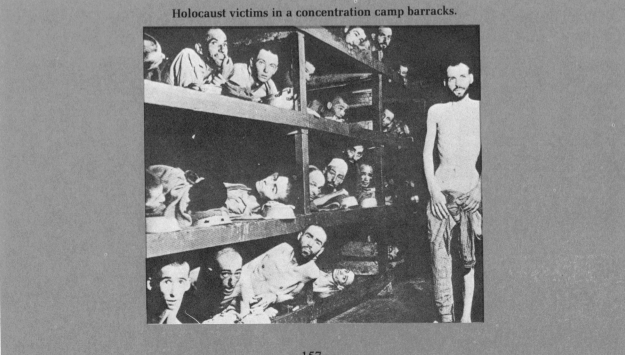

Holocaust victims in a concentration camp barracks.

Two female Jewish resistance fighters caught by the Nazis. They were executed on the spot.

fight back—who did resist their captors.

One of the events we especially remember is the uprising of the Warsaw Ghetto. Many Jews lived in the Warsaw Ghetto in Poland. They were forced to live there by the Nazi soldiers. The Nazis had conquered Poland. The Jews were very crowded. There was not enough food. Many people got sick and died. The Nazis hoped that all the Jews in the ghetto would die. Then they would not have to send them to death camps to be killed. But the Jews did not lose their hope or courage. Most of them did not die. They tried to lead normal lives. They even set up schools in the ghetto so that the children could continue to learn.

The Nazis saw that the Jews were not dying. So they decided to kill them. On the fifteenth of Nisan, the first night of Passover, the Germans marched into the Warsaw Ghetto. They were going to kill all the Jews. But the Jews had managed to smuggle in some weapons they had gotten from the underground. They fought back. Most of the Jews of the Warsaw Ghetto were killed. But many German soldiers were killed as well.

This famous photograph, taken from German archives, shows Nazi soldiers rounding up "the enemy" in the Warsaw Ghetto. The last survivors, almost unarmed, held off an armored division for many days in the heroic battle of the Warsaw Ghetto.

OBSERVANCE OF YOM HASHOAH

Many temples observe Yom Hashoah with a special service. Usually six memorial candles are lit, one for each million Jews that were killed in the Holocaust. Sometimes survivors of the Holocaust are asked to light the candles. Other times children of survivors or other members of the congregation light the candles. In some temples there is a special six-branched menorah that is lit on this day. After the candles are lit, memorial prayers are recited by the entire congregation. Often a Holocaust survivor addresses the congregation or there is a play depicting some of the terrible events of that period.

Israeli stamp honoring Jewish resistance fighters who battled against the Nazis.

In Israel, Yom Hashoah is a national day of mourning declared by the Knesset. An official ceremony takes place at *Yad Vashem*, the memorial center for the Holocaust in Jerusalem. Everyone in the country observes a moment of silence. Radio and TV stations do not broadcast their regular programs. Instead they have programs about the Holocaust all through the day.

Jews all over the world remember. Non-Jews remember too. All people of good will pray that there will never again be such a period of destruction and horror.

The Yad Vashem Memorial Museum in Israel.

This huge bronze menorah is in the Knesset courtyard in Jerusalem. It was a gift from the people of England to Israel.

Israeli stamp with a photo of the Israeli Proclamation of Statehood. It was issued to commemorate twenty-five years of Israel independence.

YOM HAATZMAUT

You just read about the saddest event in Jewish history, the Holocaust. But now you will read about one of the happiest, the establishment of the State of Israel (*Medinat Yisrael*).

For two thousand years after the destruction of Jerusalem by Rome in 70 C.E., the Jews were scattered throughout the world. They lived in many different countries. But they did not forget their homeland, Israel. They remembered it in their prayers. They sang about it and wrote poems and stories about it. They always hoped that someday Israel would again be a Jewish homeland, and that all Jews who wished to live there would be welcome.

During the Holocaust six million Jews had been killed. The vital Jewish communities in Germany, Poland, Hungary, and other countries did not exist any more. The world was shocked and horrified. The idea of a Jewish homeland in Israel was becoming more and more popular. This was something the Jews had dreamed about for two thousand years. Now it became a reality. On November 29, 1947 the General Assembly of the United Nations voted to establish the State of Israel. On May 15, 1948, the fifth day of *Iyar*, Israel officially became a nation. The Proclamation of Statehood was read. It says in part:

By virtue of the historic right of the Jewish people and the decision of the United Nations, we hereby proclaim the establishment of the Jewish State to be called the State of Israel.

HIGHLIGHTS OF ISRAELI HISTORY

Although Israel is a very young country, its short history has been filled with exciting, memorable, and sometimes sad events. Here are some of the highlights of that history:

1948: A new country is born. The State of Israel is proclaimed.

1949: Dr. Chaim Weizmann is elected President. Israel is admitted to the United Nations.

1950: 110,000 Jews from Iraq are airlifted into Israel.

1952: Itzchak Ben-Zvi is elected President.

1954: Moshe Sharett becomes Prime Minister.

1957: The first ship arrives at the port of Eilat.

1958: The Beersheba-Eilat Highway is opened.

1960: The Bar-Kochba Letters are found in the Judean Desert.

1961: The trial of Adolph Eichmann opens in Jerusalem.

1963: Zalman Shazar is elected President. Prime Minister Ben-Gurion resigns. Levi Eshkol becomes Prime Minister.

1965: The Israel Museum is opened in Jerusalem.

1966: The new Knesset building is opened in Jerusalem. S. Y. Agnon receives the Nobel Prize for Literature.

1967: Israel is victorious in the Six Day War. Jerusalem is reunited.

1968: President Shazar is re-elected for a five year term.

1969: Golda Meir becomes Prime Minister.

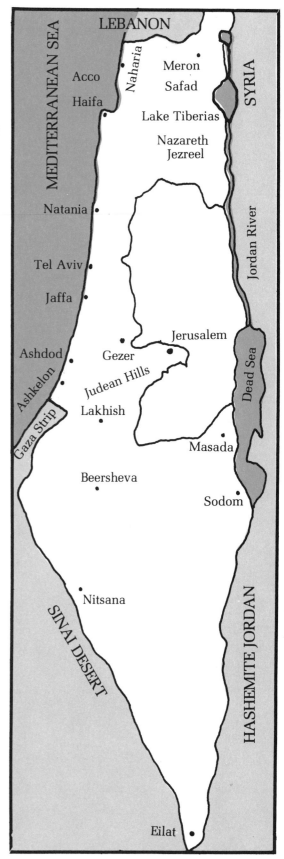

The emblem of the modern State of Israel. The ancient seven-branched Temple menorah is surrounded by olive branches. The olive branch is a symbol of peace.

1971: A new blood test for the early diagnosis of cancer is developed at Hebrew University-Haddasah Medical Center.

1972: A group of Israeli athletes go to Munich to participate in the Olympic Games. Eleven are murdered by Palestinian terrorists.

1973: Golda Meir is welcomed as a visitor at the Vatican.
Israel celebrates 25 years of independence.

1974: A Bedouin tribesman is elected as a member of the Knesset for the first time in Israel's history.

1976: Palestinian terrorists hijack a French plane with many Israelis aboard. The Israeli Army stages a successful heroic rescue at Entebbe, Uganda, where the Israelis are being held hostage.

1977: Menachem Begin is elected Prime Minister. Egyptian President Anwar Sadat visits Israel on a peace mission.

1978: Israel celebrates 30 years of independence.

A military parade in Israel on Independence Day.

CELEBRATION OF YOM HAATZMAUT

Yom Haatzmaut is Israeli Independence Day. It is observed with a great deal of festivity, both in Israel and in countries outside of Israel, on the fifth day of the Hebrew month of Iyar.

In Israel there is a gigantic parade in Jerusalem. Young people from all over the country march in this joyous event. As they march they carry banners and sing songs. This holiday is also marked by brilliant displays of fireworks and by special sporting events. But Israel's fallen heroes are not forgotten even on this happy day. Israel did not gain its independence without a struggle. Just as the colonies that became the United States had to fight for their independence in the Revolutionary War, so too did the people of Israel have to fight four wars against enemy nations before they finally had the country that was rightfully theirs. So on Independence Day, Israel remembers those who were killed fighting independence with a memorial tribute.

Israeli stamp paying tribute to David Ben-Gurion, the first Prime Minister and Minister of Defense of Israel.

The Knesset building in Jerusalem, Israel. The Knesset is the legislative body of the State of Israel. There are 120 members who are elected by a secret ballot.

Israeli stamp honoring Theodor Herzl. Herzl dedicated his life to the establishment of a Jewish State in Israel.

Independence Day, Israel remembers those who were killed fighting for Israeli independence with a memorial tribute.

In other countries there are parades and celebrations in cities that have large Jewish populations. In the United States, the biggest of all is the parade in New York down Fifth Avenue. Often more than 100,000 people, Jews and non-Jews from all over the country, come to New York on the fifth of Iyar to celebrate this joyous occasion.

Both Yom Hashoah and Yom Haatzmaut are very important days. The events they commemorate did not happen many thousands of years ago, but in the lifetime of people you know. Although Judaism is very old, it is also very new. It was important and meaningful to our ancestors long, long ago, but it is also important and meaningful to us in our own time.

The prayer *V'techezena Einenu* expresses the deep feeling that all Jews have for Israel.

May our eyes behold Your merciful return to Zion.
I praise God, who returns to Zion the glory of the
divine presence.

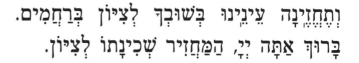

וְתֶחֱזֶינָה עֵינֵינוּ בְּשׁוּבְךָ לְצִיּוֹן בְּרַחֲמִים.
בָּרוּךְ אַתָּה יְיָ, הַמַּחֲזִיר שְׁכִינָתוֹ לְצִיּוֹן.

Israeli stamp with photo of the Knesset building in Jerusalem. The Knesset is the legislative branch of the Israeli government.

SOMETHING TO THINK ABOUT

One of the ways to prevent another Holocaust is for all people to learn to live together and respect each other. This is especially hard to do when people are very different from us. What do you think that you personally can do to learn to get along better with children of all religions, colors, and national backgrounds?

ON YOUR OWN

Do some research in the library on one of the heroes listed below. Report on him or her to your class. Or write a poem, play, or composition about the hero.

Some Heroes of the Holocaust	*Some Heroes of the State of Israel*
Anne Frank	David Ben-Gurion
Rabbi Leo Baeck	Golda Meir
Hannah Senesch	Chaim Weizmann

HEBREW WORDS AND PHRASES

Below is a list of Hebrew words and phrases relating to Yom Hashoah and Yom Haatzmaut. See how many you can learn.

Hebrew	Transliteration	Meaning
יוֹם־הַזִּכָּרוֹן	**Yom Hazikaron**	Day of Remembrance
שׁוֹאָה	**Shoah**	The Holocaust
יוֹם הַשּׁוֹאָה	**Yom Hashoah**	Holocaust Memorial Day
נִיסָן	**Nisan**	First month of Hebrew calendar
יָד־וְשֵׁם	**Yad Vashem**	Holocaust Memorial Center in Jerusalem
יוֹם הָעַצְמָאוּת	**Yom Haatzmaut**	Israel Independence Day
הַתִּקְוָה	**Hatikvah**	"The Hope" (Israel national anthem)
אִיָּיר	**Iyar**	Second month of Jewish year
מְדִינַת־יִשְׂרָאֵל	**Medinat Yisrael**	The State of Israel

The Israeli national anthem is called *Hatikvah*. The name Hatikvah means "The Hope" in Hebrew. The words were written about a hundred years ago by a young Zionist named Naphtali Herz Imber from Europe. It became the official song of the Zionist movement. Then, when Israel became a nation in 1948, Hatikvah became the national anthem of the new country. The words express how Jews everywhere feel about the land of Israel. This is what the words mean:

Naphtali Herz Imber, the composer of the Israeli national anthem, "Hatikvah."

*In the Jewish heart
A Jewish spirit still sings,
And the eyes look east
Toward Zion.*

כָּל עוֹד בַּלֵּבָב פְּנִימָה
נֶפֶשׁ יְהוּדִי הוֹמִיָּה
וּלְפַאֲתֵי מִזְרָח קָדִימָה
עַיִן לְצִיּוֹן צוֹפִיָּה.

*Our hope is not lost,
Our hope of two thousand years,
To be a free nation in our land,
In the land of Zion and
　　Jerusalem.*

עוֹד לֹא אָבְדָה תִקְוָתֵנוּ
הַתִּקְוָה שְׁנוֹת אַלְפַּיִם
לִהְיוֹת עַם חָפְשִׁי בְּאַרְצֵנוּ
בְּאֶרֶץ צִיּוֹן וִירוּשָׁלָיִם.

UNIT V
THE JEWISH LIFE-CYCLE

The circle of life goes on and on. It never ends. A baby is born. It grows up. It marries. It has babies of its own. And so the circle begins again.

You are part of that circle. Once you were a baby. Now you are a young boy or girl. You will grow up, be Bar or Bat Mitzvah, go to college, be trained for your life's work, get married, and become a parent with children of your own. It seems very far away to you now, but it will happen before you know it.

What kind of person will you be? What will your values be? How will you live? What values will you pass on to your children? These are important questions. Their answers will depend on many things. The values you learned at home. The things you learned in school. The happenings in the world as you were growing up. The friends you made and the people you met.

Jewish parents hope that their children will grow up to be good Jews. They hope that their children will learn Jewish values, marry a Jewish man or woman, have a good Jewish home, and raise their own children to be good Jews. The values you learn at home, in your temple, and in your religious school will guide you in this goal. Perhaps some of the things you have learned in this book will help you as well.

BEING BORN

Before a baby is born God decides what kind of person it will be. Will it be a man or a woman? Will it be short or tall? Will it be skinny or fat? Will it be a scholar or a musician? A poet or a banker? Then God chooses a soul for the baby.

Before the soul is joined with the body, an angel carries the soul all over the world. It teaches it all the wisdom of the ages. The angel teaches the soul all there is to know about the person whose life it will be. The soul learns all there is to know. Then it joins with the body of the baby that is about to be born.

When a baby is born it has all the wisdom and knowledge in the world. But at the moment of its birth, God touches the baby. The soul forgets everything it has learned. The baby must grow up and learn all there is to know. That takes a lifetime.

—Aggadah

The birth of a new baby is the greatest joy that can come to any family. To the new parents the life they have created represents their hope for the future. To the Jewish people it represents another Jew to carry on the great traditions of Judaism. To the world and people in general, it represents the continuation of life from generation to generation. But the baby itself is not aware of its importance. It does not know of the joy and hope it has brought. It is content to eat and sleep, be played with, and loved.

NAMING THE BABY

Our names are a very important part of who we are. Without a name we are just "he" or "she" or "hey you." With a name we are someone special. We have an "identity." We are Samuel or Susan or Anne or Sidney.

When a baby is born, it does not have a name. It is given one by its parents, who choose the name very carefully according to certain Jewish naming customs. These customs vary among different groups of Jews. Most Jewish children that you know were named in memory of a close relative who has died—usually a grandparent or a great-grandparent. That is because most Jews in this country are descended from Jews who came here from Europe. It is the custom for European or Ashkenazic Jews to name their children for a relative who has died. If you lived in Greece, Turkey, or other countries where Oriental or Sephardic Jews

The birth of a new baby is the greatest joy that can come to a family.

live, you and your friends would probably be named after close living relatives, but not your parents. If you lived in Israel your parents might have named you for an event, a place, a tree, or a flower. Or they might have made up a name that sounded pretty to them.

Most Jewish children have two first names. One is their Hebrew name. The other is their English, French, Italian, or American name as the case may be. Usually the everyday or non-Hebrew name is a translation of the Hebrew name. For example, a boy whose Hebrew name is Aryeh (which means "lion") might be called Leon, which is a form of the word "lion." A girl whose Hebrew name is Penina (which means a "pearl" in Hebrew) might be called Pearl, and so on. Sometimes the non-Hebrew name is gotten by taking the first letter of the Hebrew name and thinking of whatever name is popular at the time that begins with that letter. For example Mordecai might be translated as Murray or Mark or Morton or Morris. Sara might be Sarah or Sylvia or Simone or Sarelle.

In addition to a first name, all Jewish children have a Hebrew last name. Usually it is *ben* (son of) or *bat* (daughter of) followed by the first name of the father. In some communities ben or bat is followed by the mother's first name instead of the father's. This is the name by which the person is called to the Torah for an Aliyah. In some temples, it has recently become the practice to call a person to the Torah by following ben or bat with both the mother's and father's names.

The day on which the new baby is named is usually a very important one for the baby, the parents, and the Jewish community. Often the ceremony is followed by a party to which friends and relatives are invited. Everyone gets a chance to congratulate the parents and wish them well. Baby girls are usually named at the temple on the Shabbat following their birth.

On the eighth day after his birth, a baby boy undergoes the rite of circumcision, or *Brit Milah*. *Brit Milah* has been practiced by our people for some four thousand years.

It began in the days of Abraham. The Book of Genesis tells us: "This is My Covenant, which you shall keep, between Me and you and thy seed after thee. Every male among you shall be circumcized . . . And Abraham was ninety years old and nine, when he was circumcised."

A painting of a Brit Milah ceremony by the German Jewish artist Moritz David Oppenheim, about 1850.
In the picture we see the god mother bringing the child to the door of the syna-gogue. The mohel (performer of the circumcision) is wrapped in a large talit and waits for the newly born infant.

Most Jewish children have Hebrew names in addition to their regular names. Is this important? Why do you think so?

HEBREW WORDS AND PHRASES

Below is a list of Hebrew words and phrases relating to being born. See how many you can learn.

בֶּן	**Ben**	Son of
בַּת	**Bat**	Daughter of
פִּדְיוֹן־הַבֵּן	**Pidyon Haben**	"Redeeming of the Son" ceremony
בְּרִית־מִילָה	**Brit Milah**	Circumcision ceremony

LEARNING MORE ABOUT:
PIDYON HABEN

There is an ancient ceremony that is still observed by many Jewish families even in our own day. It is called *Pidyon Haben* and means "redeeming (buying back) the son." The history of this ceremony is very interesting.

Long, long ago when the Holy Temple stood in Jerusalem, every first-born son was pledged to serve in the Temple. If the parents did not wish for him to serve, they could redeem him from his duty to serve. This was done by paying five pieces of silver to the priest of the Temple.

The ceremony of redeeming the first-born son continued even after the Temple was destroyed. When a baby who is the first-born son of his mother is thirty days old, a short ceremony is held in which a member of the family of priests receives a sum of money symbolic of redeeming the baby. Usually the money is given to charity.

In our time many families continue this ancient tradition. Usually it is the occasion for a happy party when relatives and friends come to see the new baby.

GROWING UP

Two wise men of Chelm (who were not really very wise) were once having a conversation. How, they wondered, did a person grow? Did a person grow from the feet up or from the head down?

"Surely," said the first, "people grow from the feet up. Last year I bought my son a suit for his Bar Mitzvah and it fit just right. This year the pants are two inches above the ankle. That proves that people grow from the feet up."

"That's silly," said the second. "People grow from the head down. Last week I saw a parade. Everybody's feet were on the same level. But their heads were different heights. That proves that a person grows from the head down."

—Folk Tale

After a new baby comes home from the hospital, it needs lots of attention. It must be loved and cared for. It must be taught how to live with others in the family and how to get along with people outside the family. The parents must make sure that the child stays healthy and that it learns to become a good person. Being a mother or father is not an easy job. It requires time, patience, and self-sacrifice. But watching a child grow from a small baby into a happy and worthwhile adult is the greatest reward that can come to a parent.

A JEWISH EDUCATION

Next to taking care of the health and physical needs of a child, the parents' greatest responsibility is seeing that the child is educated. When a baby comes into the world, it does not know anything. It must learn to talk and to walk. It must learn what is safe and what is dangerous, what is pleasurable and what is painful. As it gets older, it must go to school and learn to read and write, to do math, and to understand science. Eventually the child will grow up and go to high school and college. Perhaps he or she will go to graduate school or law school or medical school or dental school. Education is a very important value in Jewish families. A very large proportion of Jewish boys and girls go to college and then to graduate or professional school.

Watching a child grow into a happy, worthwhile adult is the greatest reward that can come to a parent.

But Jewish parents are concerned with more than just the general education of their children. Jewish parents want their children to learn the values and teachings of their people. They want their children to learn Hebrew. They want them to learn the prayers and customs. They want them to learn how to be good Jews so that when they grow up they can pass the wonderful heritage of Judaism on to their own children. So most Jewish parents send their children to Hebrew or religious school.

There are different kinds of Jewish schools. Some boys and girls to to afternoon Hebrew schools. School is in session two, three, or four afternoons a week and Sunday mornings. The children learn to read and speak Hebrew. They learn prayers and Jewish customs. They learn Jewish history and Bible. Other boys and girls go to Sunday school, which meets only on Sunday mornings. There they learn prayers and Jewish customs. Still other boys and girls go to day schools where they learn general as well as Jewish subjects. A few of the schools teach Yiddish as well as Hebrew.

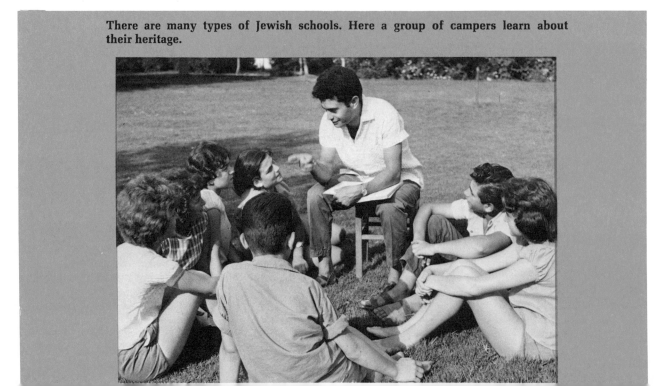

There are many types of Jewish schools. Here a group of campers learn about their heritage.

What kind of Jewish school do you go to—an afternoon Hebrew school? a Sunday school? a Jewish day school? or a Yiddish school? Whichever kind it is, you are learning to love Judaism and to make it an important part of your life. Then, when you are grown, you will be able to pass Jewish traditions on to your own children. That is how Judaism survives and stays strong.

Jewish education is for adults, too. Here, a group of adults are learning to speak Hebrew.

BAR AND BAT MITZVAH

When a Jewish child reaches the age of thirteen a very important ceremony is held. The child becomes *Bar* or *Bat Mitzvah*. In the first chapter you learned what a mitzvah is. You learned that it means "commandment." It is also used to mean all the special things we do because we are Jewish.

When you are very young, it is the responsibility of your parents to see that you lead a Jewish life. Your parents take you to temple. They teach you what is right. They show you how to observe Jewish customs and rituals. They enroll you in Hebrew school. They guide you in observing the mitzvot.

But as you become older, you become more and more responsible for your own actions. When you are thirteen, you become Bar or Bat Mitzvah. Bar means "son of." Bat means "daughter of." At thirteen, you become the son or daughter of *mitzvot*. This means that you are responsible for doing the mitzvot. You are responsible for doing those special things that make you Jewish.

A Bat Mitzvah being called to the Torah.

To mark this important day, there is a special ceremony in the temple. You are called to the *Torah* to recite the blessings and *Maftir*. Sometimes you will also read the *Haftarah* and give a sermon. Your parents, relatives, and friends are there to honor you. Usually a festive party is planned following the service.

Many of the customs of Bar and Bat Mitzvah are very new. It was very different in the days of your grandparents. In those days only boys became Bar Mitzvah. Bat Mitzvah for girls is a very recent ceremony. In your grandparents' day most girls did not go to Hebrew school. It was not considered important for them to learn Hebrew or Bible.

In our day it is different. Girls and boys go to Hebrew school together. They learn the

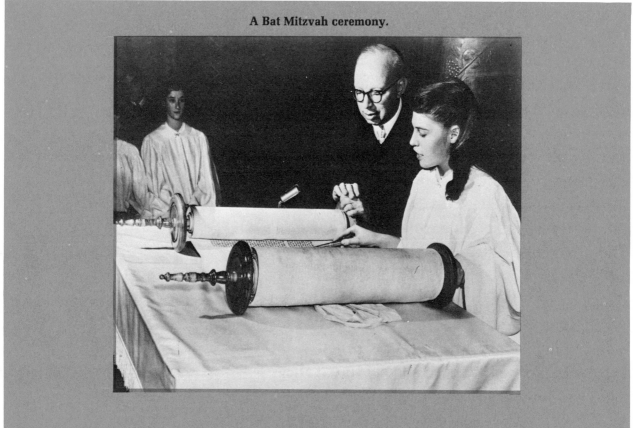

A Bat Mitzvah ceremony.

same things. Some girls grow up to become rabbis, cantors, religious-school principals and teachers, or presidents of congregations. They share equally in Jewish religious life. Bat Mitzvah is as important a religious ceremony for girls as Bar Mitzvah is for boys.

GROWING TO MANHOOD AND WOMANHOOD

The greatest joy of any parents is to see their children grow up into happy, healthy, worthwhile men and women. That is what your parents and those who love you wish for you. Someday you too will grow up, get married, have children, and teach your children to be good people and good Jews.

A ketubah (marriage contract), written in Italy, 1838. This document, listing the obligations of the bridegroom toward his bride, is written in Aramaic and must bear the signatures of two witnesses.

SOMETHING TO THINK ABOUT

What are some of the things you have learned from studying this book? How can they help you now? How can they help you as you grow up? What would you have liked to learn that you didn't? What can you do to learn more about your Jewish heritage?

ON YOUR OWN

Continue your Jewish education during your summer vacation. Read books on Jewish subjects. Go to services at the temple. Visit places of Jewish interest. Ask lots of questions.

Have a happy summer.

HEBREW WORDS AND PHRASES

Below is a list of Hebrew words and phrases relating to growing up. See how many you can learn.

בַּר־מִצְוָה	**Bar Mitzvah**	Temple ceremony for boy at age thirteen
בַּת־מִצְוָה	**Bat Mitzvah**	Temple ceremony for girl at age thirteen
מִצְווֹת	**Mitzvot**	Commandments, good deeds
תּוֹרָה	**Torah**	Five Books of Moses
מַפְטִיר	**Maftir**	Torah reading by Bar or Bat Mitzvah

INDEX

INDEX

Page references in this index include both the text
of the book and the illustration captions

הכרזה על הקמת מדינת ישראל

DECLARATION OF INDEPENDENCE
OF THE
STATE OF ISRAEL

The Land of Israel was the birthplace of the Jewish people. Here their spiritual, religious and national identity was formed. Here they achieved independence and created a culture of national and universal significance. Here they wrote and gave the Bible to the world.

Exiled from Palestine, the Jewish people remained faithful to it in all the countries of their dispersion, never ceasing to pray and hope for their return and restoration of their national freedom.

Impelled by this historic association, Jews strove throughout the centuries to go back to the land of their fathers and regain statehood. In recent decades, they returned in their masses. They reclaimed a wilderness, revived their language, built cities and villages, and established a vigorous and evergrowing community, with its own economic and cultural life. They sought peace, yet were ever prepared to defend themselves. They brought blessings of progress to all inhabitants of the country.

In the year 1897 the first Zionist Congress, inspired by Theodor Herzl's vision of a Jewish State, proclaimed the right of the Jewish people to a national revival in their own country.

This right was acknowledged by the Balfour Declaration of November 2, 1917, and reaffirmed by the Mandate of the League of Nations, which gave explicit international recognition to the historic connection of the Jewish people with Palestine and their right to reconstitute their National Home.

The Nazi holocaust which engulfed millions of Jews in Europe proved anew the urgency of the reestablishment of the Jewish State, which would solve the problem of Jewish homelessness by opening the gates to all Jews and lifting the Jewish people to equality in the family of nations.

Survivors of the European catastrophe as well as Jews from other lands, claiming their right to a life of dignity, freedom and labor, and undeterred by hazards, hardships and obstacles, have tried unceasingly to enter Palestine.

In the second World War, the Jewish people in Palestine made a full contribution in the struggle of freedom-loving nations against the Nazi evil. The sacrifices of their soldiers and efforts of their workers gained them title to rank with the people who founded the United Nations. On November 29, 1947, the General Assembly of the United Nations adopted a resolution for reestablishment of an independent Jewish State in Palestine and called upon inhabitants of the country to take such steps as may be necessary on their part to put the plan into effect.

This recognition by the United Nations of the right of the Jewish people to establish their independent state may not be revoked. It is, moreover, the self-evident right of the Jewish people to be a nation, as all other nations, in its own sovereign state.

Accordingly we, the members of the National Council, representing the Jewish people in Palestine and the Zionist movement of the world, met together in solemn assembly by virtue of the natural and historic right of the Jewish people and of the resolution of the General Assembly of the United Nations, hereby proclaim the establishment of the Jewish State in Palestine, to be called Israel.

We hereby declare that as from the termination of the Mandate at midnight this night of the 14th to 15th of May, 1948, and until the setting up of duly elected bodies of the State in accordance with a Constitution to be drawn up by a Constituent Assembly not later than the first day of October, 1948, the present National Council shall act as the Provisional State Council, and its executive organ, the National Administration shall constitute the Provisional Government of the State of Israel.

The State of Israel will promote the development of the country for the benefit of all its inhabitants; will be based on precepts of liberty, justice and peace taught by the Hebrew prophets; will uphold the full social and political equality of all its citizens without distinction of race, creed or sex; will guarantee full freedom of conscience, worship, education and culture; will safeguard the sanctity and inviolability of shrines and holy places of all religions; and will dedicate itself to the principles of the Charter of the United Nations.

The State of Israel will be ready to cooperate with the organs and representatives of the United Nations in the implementation of the resolution of November 29, 1947, and will take steps to bring about an economic union over the whole of Palestine.

We appeal to the United Nations to assist the Jewish people in the building of its state and admit Israel into the family of nations.

In the midst of wanton aggression we call upon the Arab inhabitants of the State of Israel to return to the ways of peace and play their part in the development of the state, with full and equal citizenship and due representation in all its bodies and institutions, provisional or permanent.

We offer peace and amity to all neighboring states and their peoples, and invite them to cooperate with the independent Jewish nation for the common good of all. The State of Israel is ready to contribute its full share to the peaceful progress and reconstitution of the Middle East. Our call goes out to the Jewish people all over the world to rally to our side in the task of immigration and development, and to stand by us in the great struggle for the fulfillment of the dream of generations — the redemption of Israel.

With trust in Almighty God, we set our hands to this declaration at this session of the Provisional State Council in the city of Tel Aviv this Sabbath eve, the fifth day of Iyar, 5708, the fourteenth day of May, 1948.

PHOTOGRAPHIC CREDITS

American Jewish Committee, British Museum; Brooklyn Museum; Cairo Museum; Cliche des Musees Nationaux, Paris, France; Cordova Museum, Spain; Department of Antiquities, Jerusalem, Israel; Hebrew Immigrant Aid Society; Hebrew Union College; Jewish Museum, New York; Jewish Theological Seminary, New York; Library of Congress; Metropolitan Museum of Art; Morgan Library; Oriental Institute, University of Chicago; Palphot, Israel; Staatliche Museen, Berlin; Toledo Museum, Spain; University Museum, The, University of Pennsylvania; YIVO, Yiddish Institute for Jewish Research; Zionist Archives, New York.